D1572310

The Muse
of Abandonment

The Muse
of Abandonment

Origin, Identity, Mastery
in Five American Poets

Lee Upton

Lewisburg
Bucknell University Press
London: Associated University Presses

Associated University Presses
440 Forsgate Drive
Cranbury, NJ 08512

Associated University Presses
16 Barter Street
London WC1A 2AH, England

Associated University Presses
P.O. Box 338, Port Credit
Mississauga, Ontario
Canada L5G 4L8

The paper used in this publication meets the requirements of the American National Standard for Permanence of Paper for Printed Library Materials Z39.48-1984.]

Library of Congress Cataloging-in-Publication Data

Upton, Lee, 1953–
    The muse of abandonment : origin, identity, mastery in five American poets / Lee Upton.
        p.   cm.
    Includes bibliographical references and index.
    ISBN 0-8387-5396-5 (alk. paper)
    1. American poetry—20th century—History and criticism.
2. Alienation (Social psychology) in literature. 3. Power (Social sciences) in literature. 4. Identity (Psychology) in literature.
5. Liberty in literature. 6. Wright, Charles, 1935–   —Criticism and interpretation. 7. Glück, Louise, 1943–   —Criticism and interpretation. 8. Tate, James, 1943–   —Criticism and interpretation. 9. Valentine, Jean—Criticism and interpretation.
10. Edson, Russell—Criticism and interpretation. I. Title.
PS310.A44U67   1998
811'.5409353—dc21
                                                                98-12153
                                                                CIP

Contents

Acknowledgments

I wish to express my gratitude to the editors of those journal in which some of this material appeared in different form. Portions of the chapter on Charles Wright were published in *Poesis: A Journal of Criticism*. Portions of the chapters on Russell Edson and James Tate appeared in the *South Atlantic Review,* under the editorship of Robert F. Bell, whose comments were unfailingly astute.

I am grateful to those authors from whom I requested permission to reprint their poems: Russell Edson, James Tate, and Jean Valentine. Each of them responded promptly and generously to my requests. My gratitude extends as well to Rishi Agrawal of Ecco Press.

I wish to thank Jeffrey Bader, associate provost and director of research, and the Academic Research Committee at Lafayette College for a grant to cover permissions fees.

Randall Knoper made useful suggestions regarding an early draft of the material on James Tate, and I am grateful.

The librarians at Lafayette College have been very helpful. I wish to extend special thanks to Janemarie Berry, Betsy Moore, and Richard Everett.

Jill Riefenstahl—a model of patience and wry wit—assisted in the preparation of the manuscript.

It is a pleasure to work for the second time with Mills F. Edgerton Jr., director of Bucknell University Press, and with Julien Yoseloff, director of Associated University Presses. Christine Retz shepherded my manuscript with great care through production. Wyatt Benner once again proved to be a meticulous copy editor.

I am thankful for the continued friendship of Patricia Donahue, Bin Ramke, Sylvia Watanabe, and Bill Osborn.

My greatest debt is to my family. Cecilia's impending birth put spurs on this project. Theodora's humor and grace eased—and continue to ease—

the days. My husband, Eric J. Ziolkowski, read this manuscript more than once, never complaining despite many other demands on his time, and always offering inventive advice and sustaining encouragement. This book is dedicated to him with love, gratitude, and admiration.

Grateful acknowledgment is made to individuals and publishers who gave permission to reprint copyrighted material:

Excerpts from *Black Zodiac* by Charles Wright. Copyright © 1997 by Charles Wright. Reprinted by permission of Farrar, Straus & Giroux, Inc.

Excerpts from *Chickamauga* by Charles Wright. Copyright © 1995 by Charles Wright. Reprinted by permission of Farrar, Straus & Giroux, Inc.

Excerpts from *The World of the Ten Thousand Things: Poems 1980–1990* by Charles Wright. Copyright © 1990 by Charles Wright. Reprinted by permission of Farrar, Straus & Giroux, Inc.

"Invisible Landscape," "Clear Night," "Reunion," "Homage to Ezra Pound," "Homage to Arthur Rimbaud" from *Country Music: Selected Early Poems,* 2d ed. by Charles Wright. Copyright © 1991 by Charles Wright. Wesleyan University Press, by permission of University Press of New England.

"The Ceremony," "Journey for an Old Fellow," "His House," "The Adventures of a Turtle," "The Reason Why the Closet-Man is Never Sad," "The Cottage in the Woods," "The Long Picnic," "The Rooming House Dinner," "Erasing Amyloo," "The Unscreamed Scream," "The Ornament," "A Man Who Makes Tears" from *The Reason Why the Closet-Man is Never Sad* by Russell Edson. Copyright © 1977 by Russell Edson, Wesleyan University Press, by permission of University Press of New England.

"The Tunnel" from *The Wounded Breakfast* by Russell Edson. Copyright © 1985 by Russell Edson, Wesleyan University Press, by permission of University Press of New England.

"The Broken Daughter," "Vomit" from *The Clam Theater* by Russell Edson. Copyright © 1973 by Russell Edson, Wesleyan University Press, by permission of University Press of New England.

"Poem of Intention," "Conjugal," "The Birthday Party," "The Bride of Dream Man," "The Traveler," "Counting Sheep," "Toward the Writing" from *The Intuitive Journey and Other Works* by Russell Edson. Copyright © 1976 by Russell Edson. Reprinted by permission of Russell Edson.

"Doctor House" from *A Stone is Nobody's* by Russell Edson. Copyright © 1961 by Russell Edson. Reprinted by permission of Russell Edson.

"One Man's Story" from *The Prose Poem: An International Journal.* Copyright © 1991 by Russell Edson. Reprinted by permission of Russell Edson.

"The Couples," "Separation," "Pilgrims," "Fireside," "Orpheus and Euridice" from *Pilgrims* by Jean Valentine. Copyright © 1969 by Jean Valentine. Reprinted by permission of Jean Valentine.

Acknowledgments 9

Excerpts from *Dream Barker* by Jean Valentine. Copyright © 1965 by Jean Valentine. Reprinted by permission of Yale University Press.

Excerpts from *The Messenger* by Jean Valentine. Copyright © 1979 by Jean Valentine. Reprinted by permission of Farrar, Straus & Giroux, Inc.

Excerpts from *Ordinary Things* by Jean Valentine. Copyright © 1974 by Jean Valentine. Reprinted by permission of Farrar, Straus & Giroux, Inc.

"Snow Landscape, in a Glass Globe," from *Home Deep Blue* by Jean Valentine. Copyright © 1988 by Jean Valentine. Reprinted by permission of Alice James Books.

"Ikon," "Skate," "Seeing You," "Butane," "At the Door," "Spring and its Flowers," "Redemption," "Confluence," "To a Young Poet," "My Mother's Body, My Professor, My Bower," "The Free Abandonment Blues" from *The River at Wolf* by Jean Valentine. Copyright © 1992 by Jean Valentine. Reprinted by permission of Alice James Books.

"Happy as the Day is Long," "Autosuggestion: USS North Carolina," and "In My Own Backyard" from *Worshipful Company of Fletchers* by James Tate. Copyright © 1994 by James Tate. Reprinted by permission of The Ecco Press.

"The Wild Cheese," "Poem for the Sandman," "Nobody's Business," "Yellow Newspaper and a Wooden Leg," "Poem to Some of My Recent Poems," "Tragedy's Greatest Hits," "Mystic Moments," "Nausea, Coincidence," and "Tell Them   Was Here" from *Constant Defender* by James Tate. Copyright © 1983 by James Tate. Reprinted by permission of The Ecco Press.

"Time X," "Goodtime Jesus," "The Life of Poetry," and "Nature Poem: Demanding Stiff Sentences" from *Riven Doggeries* by James Tate. Copyright © 1973, 1975, 1976–79 by James Tate. Reprinted by permission of The Ecco Press.

"The Expert" from *Distance from Loved Ones* by James Tate. Copyright © 1990 by James Tate, Wesleyan University Press, by permission of University Press of New England.

"Awkward Silence" and "A Voyage from Stockholm to Take Advantage of Lower Prices on the Finnish Island of Aland" from *Viper Jazz* by James Tate. Copyright © 1976 by James Tate, Wesleyan University Press, by permission of University Press of New England.

"The List of Famous Hats" and "The Chaste Stranger" from *Reckoner* by James Tate. Copyright © 1986 by James Tate, Wesleyan University Press, by permission of University Press of New England.

"Intimidations of an Autobiography," "Tragedy Comes to the Bad Lands," "The Lost Pilot" from *The Lost Pilot* by James Tate. Copyright © 1967 by James Tate. Reprinted by permission of James Tate.

"Wait for Me," "My Great Great Etc. Uncle Patrick Henry," "The Boy" from *Absences* by James Tate. Copyright © 1972 by James Tate. Reprinted by permission of James Tate.

"Little Yellow Leaf," "Poem," "Dear Reader," "The Initiation" from *The Oblivion Ha-Ha* by James Tate. Copyright © 1970 by James Tate. Reprinted by permission of James Tate.

"Still Life," "The Undertaking," "All Hallows," Gretel in Darkness" from *The House on Marshland*. "The Drowned Children" from *Descending Figure*. "The Triumph of Achilles" and "Mock Orange" from *The Triumph of Achilles*. All included in *The First Four Books of Poems* by Louse

Introduction

The poets considered in this study—Charles Wright, Russell Edson, Jean Valentine, James Tate, and Louise Glück—register the tremors of the contemporary exhaustion of universals and a conflicted desire for authenticating presences, a desire that is regularly frustrated in their writings. Their poetry reflects on their choice to abandon, albeit with a degree of uncertainty, abstractions that have been repeatedly assailed in postmodernism: among them, origins, identity, and mastery. Their most important poems record their sense of cultural alienation. In their lonely and at times nearly hermetic conjectures, these poets counter the solidification of any sense of selfhood founded on absolute origins. They return us to the ardor of speculation and a disciplined suspicion of public identities. We might see these poets as balanced between the delights of motion and of ahistoricity (the poem, in Emerson's words, as "conveyance") and, conversely, a lingering sense of deprivation, a personal and cultural experience of abandonment.

The archaic roots of the word *abandon* are from Old French: *a* meaning "at" or "to" and *bandon*, meaning "ban, proscription, authoritative order, jurisdiction, control, disposal, discretion" *(Oxford English Dictionary)*. Thus the term as it has evolved is double-edged, Lawrence Lipking points out, suggesting on the one hand the giving over of self to another's control and, on the other, an absolute freedom. As Lipking notes in *Abandoned Women and Poetic Tradition:* "Originally it [abandonment] signified a submission to power, as in bowing to the will of a monarch; the person who owns you can toss you away. But the same etymology, with a slight adjustment of the preposition, allows a totally opposite meaning: freedom from bondage."[1] The work of the poets discussed in this study is inscribed with the double meanings that attach themselves to abandonment: the powerlessness of being rendered subject (particularly to cultural forms of perception and cognition) and, at the same time, the experience of exuberant release from the control

11

of others, an audacious experience of isolation, even a dissolution of identity boundaries.

I have used the word *muse* in the title of this book although I recognize its anomalousness in the context of postmodern poetry. As Mary K. DeShazer observes, "It may seem strange in this postmodernist age to be speaking of the muse, that apparently antiquated notion, but as we shall see, modern poets, women and men, continue to write about 'the muse' as a central part of their creative endeavors."[2] In the case of the five poets examined here, the poem or prose poem is not simply willed but emerges through powers other than rational ones, and the source of the inspiring energy that creates the poem is allied to abandonment—not only to desertion by loved ones but to the disintegration of mythologies of presence in the midst of rapid contemporary social and technological change. Edson writes, "The sense that all is passing away, even as I write this, that in a way the *new* means death: this sense creates the Angel of Joy, which is for me the true Muse."[3] He makes unhappiness the paradoxical source of happiness, prompting the pleasures of composition. While Edson briefly figures an Angel of Joy, generally the muse is not figured for these poets. Nor is the muse met; these poets explore images of withdrawal or abandonment by what they hope to be an enlivening other. The gendering and the figuring of inspiration seem most often absent—or, at most, parodied, as when in "Toward the Writing" Edson advises writers to acquire a dead mouse for inspiration. Of these poets, Wright perhaps comes closest to conventional representations of a muse in his longings for the great literary dead, but largely the muse in all of these poets, as vitalizing force, is anticipated most fully as psychic material predicated on desertion. These poets offer variations on tradition, linking the muse to a post-Freudian sense of split being. Earlier meanings of the muse are retained in references to a source beyond conscious control, but this muse of abandonment is posed culturally, seldom as an ahistorical force. For these poets, the poem arrives from psychic compulsions shaped at some level by the compulsions of history and culture.

These five poets are models of independence, and none was appropriated by the reigning aesthetic camps of over a decade ago: the new formalists or the language poets. Instead, they have been placed in the generation defined by Stan Sanvel Rubin as the postconfessionals, a generation "dedicated to giving meaningful shape to language, but wary of too easy a celebration of the creative powers of the poet."[4] Among postconfessional attributes, according to Rubin, "The 'I' is cast into suspicion"; the self "as the source of ultimate discovery" is viewed with "tentativeness";[5] and "the self seems as much a danger as a promise."[6] Quieter in some ways than many of their contemporaries (even Tate projects a strain of buoyancy that never fully assumes didacticism), these poets of the generation born between 1934 and 1943 seemingly critique culture from a position of relative privilege. Wright and Tate studied at the Iowa Writers' Workshop; Edson for a short time at a more experimental locus of creative energy, Black Mountain College. Valentine was educated at Radcliffe, and Glück was trained in poetry workshops at Sarah Lawrence and Columbia. They began writing seriously during the Vietnam War and the civil rights movement. All these poets have participated to varying degrees in what Charles Bernstein has called "official culture"; major awards are represented in the vitas of Wright, Valentine, Tate, and Glück, among them the Yale Series of Younger Poets (Valentine and Tate), the Pulitzer Prize (Tate and Glück), and the National Book Award (Tate and Wright). Although Edson has been less often given awards than these other poets, he is regarded as "the leading practitioner of the prose poem since Char and Ponge,"[7] and much of his work has been published by Wesleyan, one of the most highly respected of university presses and the publisher of a good deal of the poetry of Wright and Tate.

In determining for these poets lines of influence, however broken, at least oblique references to Emily Dickinson have proven inevitable. Each of these poets is in some ways influenced by her example, particularly by her stylistic condensations, her omission of context, her antipathy to settled patterns of belief, and her sensitivity to the point of view of the powerless. Dickinson is the poet of the sublime detached from allegiance to institutionalized religion or a stable philosophical viewpoint. As Lipking argues, "The strength that readers have never denied Dickinson, the miraculous energy and virtuosity of her style, is related to her sense of abandonment."[8] Her eccentricity and her isolation—and her reveries on abandonment— serve as keys in very different registers in the North American heritage of these poets. Wright has pointed out that Dickinson "is the poet who, to this day, remains the only one who has ever 'spoken' to me, the only poet who, when I read her, I feel as though I understand, I know, and have heard before, somewhere."[9] Edson pursues Dickinson's radical experimentation, her punning and investigation of the interiority of words. The faint draft of sacrilege that we detect in some of her poetry becomes a gale in Edson's. Valentine credits Dickinson as a major influence on her poetry.[10] For her part, Glück admires Dickinson as "a poet of private anguish" whose "intensity and concerns speak of the crucial, not the interesting,"[11] characteristics and preoccupations that are Glück's own. As Henry Hart insightfully points out, Glück, like her predecessor, "hones a religious imagination wavering between iconoclasm and orthodoxy, worldliness and transcendence."[12] In his turn, Tate is keenly aware of Dickinson's influence on contemporary poetry—an influence with which he chooses to sport. In Tate's poem "Thoughts While Reading *The Sand Reckoner*" Dickinson proves a source of comic failure rather than revelation. His poem ends with the motif of the uncertain psychological quest, a quest that had been sustained by Dickinson. These poets' debt to their nineteenth-century predecessor (as, in part, a patron of self-effacement) seems not to signal the anxiety that Harold Bloom writes of as implicit in much influence ("the horror-of-origins that seems to be one of the most basic of human anxieties").[13] Their apparent freedom from anxiety in regard to Dickinson may be due at least in part to their perception of their predecessor as permanently estranged and estranging. In turn, their relative freedom from anxiety may reflect their self-consciousness about a contemporary American search for literary origins that is fruitfully problematic and necessarily ongoing.[14]

The poets examined in the following chapters continue the modernist project of disrupting the first-person pronoun, a project that, as Dennis Brown suggests, remains "a continuing struggle rather than a completed revolution."[15] Instead of the "extinction of personality" that Eliot called for in "Tradition and the Individual Talent," these poets more clearly reflect the psychic ramifications for individuals without hope of sacred reinvestment or cultural rescue. They are engaged in continuing the modernist project of dismantling the stable self, but with essential differences from the modernists; that is, they abrade the authority of any version of the past that might suggest an original fiction from which to mount claims of identity and mastery, and they refuse to promote a select vision of "luminous" moments within various world traditions that we find in both Pound and Eliot, or of the special stature of selfhood that we observe, for instance, in the confessional poets. The self's identity—its claims to significant and relatively stable public meaning and to "characteristic" attributions—is subject to seemingly constant revisions.

Most often, the poets analyzed here recast the confessional poem in their representations of selves, refusing the identification between the poet and the poem of many of the confessional poets and their followers, and rebuking the ideal of "sincerity." Robert Phillips emphasizes the confessional poets' fascination with poetic sincerity[16] and recovery of selfhood[17]—both of which are problematized further by these five poets; sincerity is doubted because of their post-Freudian acknowledgment of a split between the conscious and the unconscious and their conception of the extreme instability of language in representation.

Surely their stance toward "sincerity" nevertheless baffles some readers. James McCorkle argues against Charles Altieri and Mary Kinzie's charges that contemporary poetry favors "a self-indulgent expressive mode generated from the romantics."[18] McCorkle himself favors the poetry of sincerity, arguing that "the personal voice, including all its ironic and self-conscious moments, is in fact subversive, for it refutes a commodities-based culture and importantly asks for our participation and intimate connection."[19] The voices of these poets, however, even when seeming superficially sincere—that is, presented without irony and in a form that takes its conventions from realism—less often ask for the direct immediate connection with readers that McCorkle stipulates and may assume a distance that is at points adversarial. As for the "recovery of self" sought by some confessional poets, these five poets, already obsessed by doubts of a unitary self, find that even while trawling for memories through the process of writing poetry (as in Wright) they cannot anticipate establishing representations of complex psychic coherence. Memory and selfhood are both cast as inherently unreliable, and selfhood and the identity by which we formulate its public properties are subject to obscure disruptions.

We might note that in much confessional poetry the self attains tragic or near tragic stature. Even if selfhood is multivoiced, it is largely mythologized, and the identity projected in the poem's foreground holds inherent interest. In the poems under discussion, however, the mythology of self, while it may be deployed, revolves around an absent center; the question of doubt, including doubt of the self's substantiality and stability, relentlessly enters this poetry. Whereas the confessional poets greeted exposure of taboos or extreme shifts in self-representation with exhilaration, the general tone of the poets discussed here offers nearly a corrective to confessionalist extremes; their poems appear against a broad cultural backdrop in which selfhood may be seen as in the throes of artificiality and the ceaseless interplay of contemporary fictions and illusions.

The confessional poets, committed in large measure to versions of autobiography, were apt to attempt, as Robert Phillips argues, to destroy or exorcise the demonic: "All confessional art, whether poetry or not, is a means of killing the beasts which are within us, those dreadful dragons of dreams

and experiences that must be hunted down, cornered, and exposed in order to be destroyed."[20] While Phillips's argument seems to hold true for
many confessional *poems*, particularly some of those written by Plath and
Sexton, the contemporary poets on whom this study focuses are more skeptical about the possibility of eliminating psychic material. These poets are
less sanguine than the confessional poets about extracting negative psychic
complexes from even the provisional selves that they erect, perhaps because they sense an intractable continuum between personal and cultural
traumas as these are coded in language. The irritation embedded in these
poetries is both personal and cultural and seemingly impossible to dislodge
through confessionalist incantation.

I will suggest, especially regarding Edson (a poet often believed to write
from a free-floating, contrary universe submerged in the unconscious), that
these poets are critics of culture as it manifests itself in language through
which we posit identity. The seemingly reckless wit and verbal play of a
Tate poem, for instance, investigates inadequate social structures founded
on displays of authoritative self-consistency. All these poets reflect, even if
sometimes obliquely, upon coercion of thought and behavior in contemporary culture. Their strategies for achieving even a momentary sense of in-
wardness, a psychic privacy, are meant to outwit a commercialized sense of
being, a sentimentalized, ultimately reactive, and avid consumer self that is
predicated by late-twentieth-century culture in North America.

These poets' surrealist inheritance may be observed in their disruptions of time and space and in their willingness to engage extreme images,
to conflate reference areas, and to shift speech registers. Yet even as they
appear at ease with that inheritance, they are suspicious of such ease and
not apt to value all productions of the unconscious. Surrealism is seen as an
inevitability—a movement at least superficially absorbed by the culture—
albeit a deeply significant inevitability. Their allegiance is less to the doc-
trines of surrealism than to revealing what Edson calls the "hidden life"[21] as
its tentacles rise into the shared life of language shaped by public institutions. And while each of these poets has in turn absorbed elements of deep-
image poetics (an offshoot of surrealism), their work is not dependent on
primordial images, and they do not evoke what Paul Breslin isolates as "the
single most important rule in deep image poetics": "quest for union with
the unconscious."[22] The poets discussed in the following chapters complicate any such quest and intimate that the assumption of a total connection
with a Jungian unconscious may be regressive. They are attracted to repre-

sentations of unconscious processes (oblivion in Glück or melancholy in Tate and Wright; the preoedipal in Valentine or idlike cruelties in Edson) but they do not romanticize the unconscious. And although they work with a field of images to which they frequently return, they often question their own images' substantiality, deflating deep-imagist portentousness. Each of them presents the image as constructed; that is, they self-consciously point to the artificiality of their images. Wright draws in other poetics and varying philosophies to destabilize his images and to subvert his direct statements. While he often repeats seemingly elemental images, Edson does not invest them with sacred importance. He desacralizes his images while literalizing social formulae. Other striking effects that complicate our reception of these five poets' images are achieved by Valentine's use of dream references as they distort daytime anxieties rather than reveal mythic "truth," by Tate's radical condensation of dreamlike sensory materials, and by Glück's casting of distrust upon even her most impassioned speakers and the descriptives they use to embody their situations.

In resisting some aspects of the confessionalist mode—even while focusing, at points, on trauma and a strained (and straining) subjectivity, and while skeptical of any simple allegiance to surrealist extremes and deep-imagist unions—these poets chart their suspicions of self-representation. Their relation to autobiography is especially complex. Although Wright has written a good number of poems called "self-portraits," he aims for what he calls "impersonal autobiography," poems "personally impersonal as a spider's web."[23] Some of his restlessness, his penchant for stylistic games—writing a poem with no verbs and so on—arises from his dissatisfaction with fictions of a unitary self that his speakers sometimes fear are actualities. Edson, the least autobiographical of these poets, is frankly contemptuous of the autobiographical impulse. He has written of his disdain for "the empty mirror of soliloquy, the 'I' poem, where the poet can't get past himself," describing the autobiographical poem as a form of "middle-class mercantile morality."[24] For Valentine, autobiography is rendered problematic by her enactments of psychological fusion between individuals and by her rendering of personalities that are more permeable in her work than conventional autobiography allows. On his part, Tate finds the autobiographical impulse to be prematurely limiting. He magnifies the conventions of autobiography to reveal their status as inherently restrictive. In Glück, the impulse toward harsh judgments is applied to most narratives of selfhood, and the projected self momentarily becomes a transcendent icon, self-consciously plated by will—but an icon that the reader may readily choose to

suspect. *Ararat*, the most autobiographical of her collections, insists on forc-
ing its conclusions rather than enacting an ongoing ritual of confessional
revelation, and Glück's personae resist "worldly" judgments of individual
worth.

In an anguished updating of Eliot, Vernon Shetley has argued in favor
of increased difficulty in contemporary poetry. "Poetry, by bringing us to a
greater awareness of the languages by which we understand our experience, should help us resist the reduction of experience to formulas, whether
those are the formulas of lyricism or of lucidity. But to do so it will have to
be difficult."[25] The degree of difficulty in the work of these five poets varies
considerably, but each poet unsettles common reading habits and disturbs
conventional notions of the stability of the author and his or her authority.
The difficulty we may perceive in these poets' work is due in part to their
reliance on images unmediated by explanatory context. As I have already
noted, the image may seem to be suddenly ruptured or dissolved—or, in
contrast, implacably solidified—as if sensory imprints, particularly visual
imprints, are subject to either sudden evaporations or wholesale reifications
in contemporary culture as it commodifies our sense of actuality. Even Wright,
a poet who has written many long poems, is known for compressed imagistic repetitions, his sensory particles betraying his lasting attraction to the
resonant and riddling image. Glück, arguably the most lucid of these poets,
reverses conventional judgments in her implosive poems to the point that
Greg Kuzma, in what strikes me as a wrongheaded but strangely fascinating review, has charged her with "bullying" her readers.[26] Glück's antipathy
to community and communal feeling accounts in part for the sensation of
complexity that many readers perceive in her work. While her language
has remained spare and her syntax relatively unelaborate, the depth of in-
sinuation in her poetry, accomplished in part by her reliance on the
unexplicated image, complicates any ready perspective.

These are, for the most part, "anti-epiphanic" writers—a term I bor-
row from Alan Williamson, who applies it in a negative sense.[27] I would like
to employ the term in a more positive manner, for the cultural situation in
which transcendent meaning is not only undisclosed but in which attention
to the epiphanic is held suspect is projected by these poets in intriguing
ways. While these poets' personae may struggle toward provisional moments of transcendence, they most often portray themselves as waiting for
epiphany without satisfaction. The moment of failed epiphany occurs regu-

larly enough in this poetry to be considered paradigmatic. Speakers are abandoned by the transcendental figure or the cultural authority that would invest their receptivity with sacred or at least overriding importance. In varied ways, each of these poets writes of the thwarted rescue, the failed meeting, the unfulfilled ideal; the inherited structures of meaning are inscribed as faltering, although a longing for certainty and for a sustaining variety of transcendence still operates within their work.

The way movement in physical space is described in the work of these poets mirrors their psychological predicaments, most clearly their fascination with the "anti-epiphanic" situation. Wright, as we shall see in chapter 1, invests in vertical movements, ascents and descents that mark the extremes of his spiritual longings. Edson's poems unreel horizontally, as narrative is swiftly impelled along an irreversible track in which language conventions are brought to an inevitable conclusion in violence. In Valentine, movement occurs as if phenomena were to be permeated and irradiated, and as if the self were subject to violations that menace understanding. Tate's poems focus on the fractious kinesthesias of his speakers, who, as in the flight of the lost pilot (the title figure of his first book), orbit ceaselessly or travel toward ever-receding destinations. Glück frequently figures the absence of movement, a paralysis endured by her personae. Alternately, her poems may seemingly push backward toward fictions of origins, particularly fictions about the family as the source of psychic trauma.

Perhaps inevitably, the place markers of identity—homes and names—prove generative for these poets. While Wright houses himself in his fidelity to landscape, the four other poets in this study have more ambivalent relations to conceptions of home, often registering dislocation from the powerful sense of shelter that the image of home traditionally evokes. As we shall see in chapter 2, Edson creates narratives in which houses are oppressive structures, implying that the very same oppression haunts the nuclear families that inhabit such houses. Tate's speakers arrive at homes that are empty or that fragment before them; Valentine's speakers overtly state their need for shelter even while they trouble notions of stable boundaries; Glück's early speakers cannot find a home that is not built on "marshland" and sinking toward oblivion. These poets register an escape from identity, from tribalisms or belonging, whether figured in homes or in names. In Wright's catalogs of divines, names are used as supplications—denoting absence and emptiness. In Tate, we see identities encoded in nomenclature that refers to ineffectuality and that points to the impossibility of redemptive action. In

the near mysticism of Valentine, the bizarre narrations of Edson, and the austere testimonials of Glück, names are abraded, and, as we shall see, the very
act of naming (the poet's traditional impulse and task) signals some form of
desertion.

The Muse
of Abandonment

1

The Doubting Penitent: Charles Wright's Epiphanies of Abandonment

Charles Wright is one of our contemporary poets most willing to make self-characterizations for readers. Consider two statements from his prose assemblage "Bytes and Pieces":

> I write from the point of view of a monk in his cell. Sometimes I look at the stones, sometimes I look out the window.[1]

> I would like my poems to be like visionary frescoes on the walls of some out-of-the-way monastery.[2]

Surely Wright's presentation of a monk in his cell detailing his environment evokes an image of the poet as a solitary ascetic. In turn, his reference to the placement of his "visionary frescoes" indicates his fascination with the obscure and the hidden, the "out-of-the-way" phenomena that he believes will allow him to intuit spiritual presence. Throughout his career, Wright has been a self-described penitent, a pilgrim (a common persona in his poems) unvisited by the spiritual presences he seeks and unable to master his spiritual yearnings. He composes his poems with the stubborn will of a man intent on continuing his life's work without being understood by others.[3]

Wright's preoccupations are the traditional ones of the lyric poet: nature, mortality, and spiritual impulse. But he has taken these preoccupations and treated them in increasingly intricate ways; by the late 1970s he was widening and fanning out his poems as he questioned the stability of memory, identity, and language. What remains most significant in his prose writings and in oblique references within poems is his preoccupation with creating an autobiography. Such a goal is, in some ways, humble; autobiography, after all, professes to reveal primarily the limited life of its author, however well the author summons a cultural and historical situation. Yet given Wright's belief in the inherent instability of memory and language, his project is ambitious: the one life revealed in the mutable medium of language may at least covertly reflect on the ways in which language represents many lives, and his compass points of meaning are no less than the great abstractions of language, nature, and God.

Composing poetry allows Wright the hope of abandoning the limited confines of the self and "unmastering" the known, including the recognizable status of both origin and identity that Maurice Blanchot alludes to in his essay "From Dread to Language": "Most of the time, to give oneself to language is to abandon oneself. One allows oneself to be carried away by a mechanism that takes upon itself all the responsibility of the act of writing."[4] As Wright, too, suggests, the act of writing, to which he repeatedly pledges his allegiance, cannot be ultimately controlled, and the process of composition reinforces and duplicates the contours of his spiritual longings, which, similarly, remain unmastered and unsatisfied. Wright's sense of his project connects with Blanchot's argument for the intractability of words as outlined in another essay: "The writer seems to be master of his pen, he can become capable of great mastery over words, over what he wants to make them express," Blanchot writes. "But this mastery only manages to put him in contact, keep him in contact, with a fundamental passivity in which the word, no longer anything beyond its own appearance, the shadow of a word, can never be mastered or even grasped; it remains impossible to grasp, impossible to relinquish, the unsettled moment of fascination."[5] For Wright, "unmastering" is linked to his wish to dissolve into what he suggestively frames as the oblivion of belief, an ultimate union with his desires that would evaporate the limiting boundaries of selfhood and its public identity. His obsessive focus on desires that cannot be met allows him to project a poetry that he can never master; the scope of his project mandates failure rather than authority over phenomena. Yet unmastering language, paradoxically, allows Wright intense pleasure, especially the pleasure of copious writing; error and incompletion make more writing possible, prompting rewriting.

Since his early career Wright has displayed a readiness for revelation and a near-religious commitment to aesthetic discipline. His poems are suffused with spiritual reference not only derived from his upbringing in the Episcopal Church ("from which I fled and out of which I remain")[6] but from a temperamental yearning for transcendence. What we encounter in his poems are the principles and images of religious supplication and transubstantiation put in the service of language. He has called language "the most sacred place of all,"[7] arguing that the "true purpose and result of poetry" is "a contemplation of the divine" through words.[8] He describes his poems as "little prayer wheels," "wafers," "sacraments," and "hymns."[9] Yet while Wright works in a reference area of spiritual imagery, suffusing his poems with religious terminology, he resists conversion to a stable point of view of the spirit or to any one system of belief. The forms of his poems evince his continual need to experiment with questions of belief as they may be intuited through language. Over the course of his career, he has "opened" the channels of his writing to stylistic change and to conflicting, often contradictory, meditations that unsettle belief in an otherworldly power. It is as if his entertaining of doubt—doubt of deity and of language's efficacy, self-doubt and doubt of the poem itself—performed as his essential spiritual practice.

In a sense, Wright's is a faith against faith, a resistance to his early indoctrination in the Episcopal Church but not a renunciation of religious strategies for seeking transcendent meaning. He stylizes his poems in the language and impulses associated with Christianity even while he escapes from the most consequential demands of faith in a higher power. It is not too much to claim that he has spiritualized doubt; in his poems, doubt becomes particular to spiritual aspiration, for he awaits illumination despite his skepticism, which seems, in much of his poetry, a manifestation of his asceticism. Apparently the poem for Wright is a means to secure religious feeling, to attain access to something akin to ecstasy and the sensation of dissolution, however momentarily, of the limited self. It appears that it is the sensations of religious conversion that he desires, but not the trappings of corporate religious life.

Given both Wright's spiritual themes and his references to his writing practices in interviews, his critics inevitably have viewed him in saintlike terms. Alluding to the photograph of Wright on the cover of *Bloodlines*, Calvin Bedient describes the poet as "a mock frontier-saint of purity—washed in the beyond, cleaned to blankness, bouncing back brilliance."[10] David St. John notes, "For his readers, Charles Wright's poetry often serves as a kind of prayer book, a kind of poetic hymnal or speculative field guide we might carry with us on our own metaphysical journeys."[11] While I do not wish to make Wright into a caricature of a saint of any sort, it is worth noting that his persona in poems, prose, and interviews conforms in part to characteristics that William James defines as saintly: "The saintly character is the character for which spiritual emotions are the habitual centre of the personal energy." The primary qualities of the saint include, James points out, "a feeling of being in a wider life than that of this world's selfish little interests; and a conviction, not merely intellectual, but as it were sensible, of the existence of the Ideal Power";[12] "a sense of the friendly continuity of the ideal power with our own life, and a willing self-surrender to its control," "an immense elation and freedom, as the outlines of the confining selfhood melt down"; "a shifting of the emotional centre towards loving and harmonious affections."[13] Of these characteristics, Wright's frequent focus on divinity and his desire for self-surrender mark his endeavor as saintlike in James's terms. In addition, Wright is as willing as an ascetic to maintain a single-minded attention to his discipline, the discipline of probing toward intimation of divinity through experiments with language. He retains such alert mindfulness by refusing the comforts of distraction or of self-gratification and aiming for experiences linked to sainthood, particularly in terms of the disruption and dissolution of personality. His autobiographical poems in their distortions of point of view and their focus on a sketched outline of self are inflected with the contrary desire to disband selfhood entirely, in a way reminiscent of James's notion of sainthood: "Religious rapture, moral enthusiasm, ontological wonder, cosmic emotion, are all unifying states of mind, in which the sand and grit of the selfhood incline to disappear, and tenderness to rule."[14] As James sees it, this tendency toward obliteration of self-interest is paramount in sainthood: "abandonment of self-responsibility seems to be the fundamental act in specifically religious, as distinguished from moral[,] practice."[15] Sensations allied to such "abandonment" are sought repeatedly in Wright's poetry.

Inevitably, Wright's themes and vocabularies—his focus on salvation and transubstantiation, and his anticipation of impending divine presence—force his readers into a consideration of spirituality. But it is the autobiographically coded poems of an agonized speaker, a St. Sebastian punctured by the arrows of doubt, that allows for the near hagiography of some critical accounts about Wright. That is, while Wright salts his poem with allusions to otherworldly presences, it is finally his own persona, "Charles," who seems to many of his readers to be the most afflicted and ultimately spiritualized amid his pantheon. His project takes its tensions from opposing pressures, pressures between, on the one hand, salvific yearning seemingly foreordained by the depth of his early religious instruction and, on the other, by empirical rationalism ingrained upon his mind by his experiences in a secular culture.

While Wright's poems suggest, as Bedient notes, "all high church—reason's unease,"[16] at the same time—and here's one of the most prominent paradoxes in this poet's work—they battle the religious transcendence that they would evoke, particularly in a frequent trope in which the longed-for spiritual or poetic forebear fails to appear. "God is the sleight-of-hand in the fireweed, the lost / Moment that stopped to grieve and moved on . . . ," he has written and rewritten in various forms in various poems.[17] This attitude of unrewarded receptivity manifested itself immediately in Wright's career. In "Aubade," the first poem collected in his early poems in *Country Music*, his speaker is depicted as "waiting—calmly, unquestioning—for Saint Spiridion of Holy Memory to arise . . . from his grove of miracles above the hill" (*CM*, 3). Wright's speakers assume postures of expectation, however acutely aware they may be of landscape and weather. As in another early poem, "Nocturne," his speaker is already a "strayed traveller, or some misguided pilgrim" (*CM*, 6). His speaker's anticipation, however, is crossed; even if the speaker is "waiting—calmly unquestioning—" the holy figure cannot emerge. Wright is the supplicant for whom no visitation entirely makes itself known but who finds even the lack of anticipated appearance a resonant sign of mystery. In other poems, if a strange figure does arrive with the semblance of a message, as in "Journal of the Year of the Ox," the message is unsatisfying nevertheless. More often "No one comes forth. Nothing steps / Into the underbrush or rises out of the frame," as in "Local Journal."[18]

Wright's imagination longs for divine visitations and divine interventions; yearning is a generative force in his poetry. The failure to be visited by any higher power practically achieves paradigmatic status in his work. His stopping short—his hesitancy, his refusal to release skepticism—is countered by his wish to be "battered" by God, as if only an extreme fleshly violation could release the self from doubt. His poems float above simple assertions, insisting on the inexplicable, while Wright cannot abandon himself to belief. That is, abandonment of self to God is a temptation that his poems resist—almost unsuccessfully. God in this scheme may seem a destroyer and Wright the penitent who wants to be "picked clean" by the divine. His characteristic wish for self-purification, even to the point of what appears to be self-obliteration (a desire that echoes John Donne and Gerard Manley Hopkins), is contrasted with Wright's secondary voice in "Clear Night." In this poem he would ask for a miracle, even while he finds himself stubbornly limited by rational imperative and material desire as in "T'ang Notebook": "Give me a sign, / show me the blessing pierced in my side"

(*WTT*, 103). And yet, like Donne, he would be battered by his God in "Clear Night":

> I want to be bruised by God.
> I want to be strung up in a strong light and singled out.
> I want to be stretched, like music wrung from a dropped
>   seed.
> I want to be entered and picked clean.
>
> And the wind says "What?" to me.
> And the castor beans, with their little earrings of death,
>   say "What?" to me.
> And the stars start out on their cold slide through
>   the dark.
> And the gears notch and the engines wheel.
>
>   (*CM*, 152)

While the speaker wishes for a fleshly violation through the overwhelming energy of a higher power, the poem situates its spiritual cravings among natural emblems that in this context initially signal incredulity. Just the same, through the bemused question of the wind and the castor beans Wright suggests that the persona's desire is in some manner answered. His self-dispersal is put into effect at the moment of writing; his condition of existence is ultimately that of being "entered and picked clean" by forces of nature as they are energized by God's will and by the process of writing, which, for this poet, abrades certainty. For Wright, composing the poem proves a means to both record and act out the desire to be violated by divine force.

Perhaps precisely because of the destructive power that he attaches to deity, transcendence is feared by Wright, and perhaps even more feared than desired. A moment occurs in "A Journal of the Year of the Ox" that bespeaks a corollary anxiety to that of the anxiety that revolves for Wright around the failure of miraculous presence to emerge: that is, the poem registers horror at completion, a terror of being united with one's desires. In the twilight, with the voices of children near (a scene reminiscent of T. S. Eliot's "Little Gidding"), Wright's persona imagines ultimate transformation:

> The stone ball on the gate post, the snail shell in its
>   still turning—
> Would burst into brilliance at my touch.

But I sat still, and I touched nothing,
                    afraid that something might change
And change me beyond my knowing, . . .

                                        (*WTT*, 167)

He withdraws from a potentiality that threatens to absorb his identity. In this near visitation, the speaker is left with only the semblance of blazing attention. Such a scenario underscores the perceptions that we have entertained; yearning and yet doubtful, Wright prefers a posture betwixt and between the earthly and the transcendent. It is the pose to which he is accustomed and through which he most fully experiences the adventurous force of his own restless reverie.

What seems a near constant, despite or perhaps because of Wright's representations of desire for an ideal power, is his very attraction to images of disappearance. The image, for Wright, is of essential importance, and he has rightly been described by Charles Altieri as "a pure practitioner of the image."[19] Implicit in Wright's poetics of the image is a notion of the image's tenuousness: the image as revelatory of doubt, presence as paradoxical indicator of absence. "The image is always a mirror. Sometimes we see ourselves in it, and sometimes we don't." Although he has been allied with deep-image poetics, his aesthetic actually abrades the image, creating the effect of dissolving or dimming the visual field. His images hover between substance and immateriality. They are dominated by rippling or fading effects poising the images toward their own evaporation. Such images reflect his subject matter: "The image is always spiritual as it is beyond us, and analogous and seditious."[20] Unlike the deep-image poets, he does not rely on a battery of images that reflect a Jungian unconscious, but instead upon what Richard Tillinghast describes as "the dialectic between a philosophy that negates phenomena and a sensory keenness."[21] At times it is as if he is cutting free or burning his way through the rudimentary signals that lead us to establish any sort of primary visual ground. He is then a Penelope of the image, undoing what he has created and insisting on the radical instability of his images and, often enough, of the autobiographical self as reflected by images.

The image as sign of time at work is particularly compelling to Wright. Aesthetically, he favors the glimpse of Eden, the paradise out of reach and thus hauntingly seductive. In many of his poems after the mid-1970s with their descending ladders of lines that allow for white space, slow turns or

sudden descents, he reinforces through the poems' forms his thematic preoccupations with disintegrating natural and spiritual elements. He foils our
notion of simple description, just as the voices in his lyric poems fluctuate
between the earthly and the otherworldly, and embody his refusal to be
"located" to the point where even his catalogs of landscape and weather,
however meticulous, seem unearthly. "Wonder and awe must reside always
in partial obscurity,"[22] he has written, and his attraction to descriptive opacity
accounts for some of the challenge that his poems pose. Most often this
challenge involves our registering evanescence in images that we are led in
context to associate alternately with presence and absence. The poems for-
age in the past, haloed by loss and regret or—particularly in referring to
Italy, site of Wright's "discovery" of poetry—a poignant nostalgia. His ruminations on such effects are infused with frequent sideways references to
Asian philosophies and Asian poetry as well as to the vital significance of
open space in painting:

> —Exclusion's the secret: what's missing is what appears
> Most visible to the eye:
>   the more luminous anything is,
> The more it subtracts what's around it, . . .

(WTT, 122)

In turn, the image of dust reappears frequently, an allusion to the biblical
symbol of human ephemerality, but cast into contemporary scenes of desolation. In quoting Robert Hughes's discussion of the contemporary Italian
painter Giorgio Morandi, Wright might have been describing his own aesthetic: "'gradual permutations of experience, by insinuations that verge on
monotony, as the color of dust will seem monotonous until you really look
at it.'"[23]

A poet of changing optical effects, Wright connects the instability of
images cast in words with images of light: "Looming and phosphorescent
against the dark, / Words, always words" (WTT, 99). In "Cryopexy" (the
title refers to "An operation to repair, by freezing with liquid Freon glass, a
tear on the eye's retina")[24] words are light and, in turn, selfhood is light-
composed. Light and self, and the self composed of images in the poem, are
jittery as cells under the microscope:

> One black, electric blot, blood-blown,
> Vanishes like Eurydice
>   away from the light's mouth

And under the vitreous bulge of the eye's hill,
Down, O down, down . . .

(WTT, 100–101)

The lyric poet is thus an Orpheus who draws the Eurydice of the image toward the light, yet, no sooner than he looks back upon his work, must witness his images fading into darkness. The intractability of image and language—and self as language-composed—makes of the poem a Eurydice and each letter on the page, "one black, electric blot, blood-blown," and about to disappear. Blanchot is again suggestive in terms of Wright's preference for dissolving images in his poetry—particularly as his preference may prove resonant in connection with the myth of Orpheus and Eurydice:

> [I]f he [Orpheus] did not turn around to look at Eurydice, he still would be betraying, being disloyal to, the boundless and imprudent force of his impulse, which does not demand Eurydice in her diurnal truth and her everyday charm, but in her nocturnal darkness, in her distance, her body closed, her face sealed . . . not as the intimacy of a familiar life, but as the strangeness of that which excludes all intimacy; it does not want to make her live, but to have the fullness of her death living in her.[25]

Orpheus would play God; he would bring the dead to life again by means of his own miraculous powers to awaken sympathy and desire through his lyre. But Orpheus (and here we see one reason for Wright's favoring of the figure) fails; like so many of Wright's speakers he is fated to balance between life and death. While he works for the ultimate realization of his desires, Orpheus is destined to be denied, particularly through his impatience and lack of faith—and his anxious intellect that translates presence into absence.

The desire that Blanchot finds in the myth of Orpheus duplicates in a complex way Wright's desire for a death-inhabited poetry and for images, and self-portraits, that seemingly dissipate. Of the image, Blanchot suggestively argues: "Where there is nothing, that is where the image finds its condition, but disappears into it. The image requires the neutrality and the effacement of the world, it wants everything to return to the indifferent depth where nothing is affirmed, it inclines toward the intimacy of what still continues to exist in the void; its truth lies there."[26] In a manner that echoes Blanchot's formulation, Wright disrupts his own images, insisting on creating a sequence of images that are about to be released from materiality. His images of ascension and his common practice of using verbals that refer to rising actions are met almost relentlessly with images of falls, dissipations, and dissolves. It is as if when Wright turns to presence he is impelled, like Orpheus, to send what he has discovered back into the underworld of the unconscious and to inculcate in readers an obscure sense of loss.

Given the tendency of his poetry to create impressions of emptiness and silence, what human presence could penetrate Wright's poetry? As many of his readers observe, hardly so much as a single dominant human other is fully cast as a complete living personality in his poetry. Wright's epigraph to *Country Music*—"The country was always better than the people" (from Hemingway)—underscores his work as an unpeopled poetry that favors its landscapes more than any potential for describing human relationship. Persons pass through the poems anecdotally, often as solitaries, as fellow alert observers, or as the mysterious dead. Frequently they are engendered into a typology or apotheosized. The poems effect an ultimate faith in language conducted with little human contact and most often with attentiveness to catalogs of invented divines or veiled abstractions—Sister of Mercies, Our Lady of Knoxville, Madonna of Tenderness and Lady of Feints and Xs. Such names pinpoint irreality more often than human presence. As in Wallace Stevens's poetry, place conveys more meaning than any personality other than the poet's. As such, Wright's musings are almost unrelievedly solitary. He passes along the peripheries of relationship, and even his relationship with the reader, which might seem more open to the suggestion of intimacy, is troubled by the impression of solitude. For many readers, the experience of reading Wright is like that of overhearing a lone mind ruminating to itself. The work most often avoids presenting direct personal interchanges with others. That is, Wright enacts a poetry of religious sentiment in which any potential encounter with divinity is more sought after and reflected upon than is mortal presence. Indeed, his poems may seem so often unpeopled (even when listing names) in part because he prefers to pursue underworld spirits and, in connection with them, intimations about landscape and language as they have been inherited from and channeled to us by those who are now themselves dead. The dead form a "culture" of sorts for him, a culture that affects current phenomena.

In their tropes, their very catalogs, on being and nonbeing, in the spiritual lure of silence and darkness, Wright's poems bear an unmistakable signature. More often than most of his contemporaries, he is a poet of the list, practicing a conjoining of things as if he were mounting evidence of some sort. Unlike his contemporary James Tate, whose catalogs suggest spiraling (even if sometimes comic) desperation, Wright composes sequences of images that point quietly to otherworldly forms. His accumulation of often exquisite imagistic catalogs represents one of the most compelling instances of a contemporary poet uniting his sense of autobiography with his sense of language and, in turn, with his facility with the image. His fluent, seductive, mysterious images that hover as if about to evaporate reflect Wright's need to escape identity in the quixotic processes of writing: "I write poems to untie myself, to do penance and disappear" (*CM*, 141).

Wright has been referred to as a particularly difficult poet to paraphrase or describe, as Helen Vendler observes: "Because Wright's poems, on the whole, are unanchored to incident, they resist description; because they are not narrative, they defy exposition. They cluster, aggregate, radiate, add layers like pearls."[27] We may note that in Vendler's description, Wright's poems are essentially cumulative. We should note, however, that the poems, as we have seen, also "shed," discarding what they gather and pursuing, in Wallace Stevens's terms, the "Nothing that is not there and the nothing that is." Indeed, at times, images of divesting become nearly prescriptive.

Despite Wright's imagistic and thematic focus on shedding preconceptions and on "unlearning," he emphasizes the necessity of repeating his questions about the nature of divinity, as in "Dog Day Vespers": "I'm writing you now by flashlight, / The same news and the same story I've told you often before" (*WTT*, 32). Or more comically elsewhere: "There is so little to say, and so much time to say it in" (*WTT*, 72). Repetition of many sorts—of images, scenarios, statements and questions—is not only a signature device, an identifiable stylistic and conceptual element in his poetry, but, to literalize the term, repetition appears imagistically as self-inscription: "You've got to sign your name to something, it seems to me. / And so we rephrase the questions / Endlessly, / hoping the answer might somehow change" (*WTT*, 60).

In his eagerness to repeat essential scenarios, Wright's poems revisit the seductions of his introduction to poetry. He has written often of his initial encounter with poetry in spring 1959 as a twenty-four-year-old serviceman who read Ezra Pound's verse at Lake Garda while stationed in Italy. His textual "encounter" is a meeting not only with poetry but with nature, setting in motion his later preoccupation with the relationship between word and nature—and with Pound as poetic influence. By detailing Pound's influence on his own work in interviews, essays, and poems, Wright recaptures the first enchantments of his discovery of poetry and focuses on his preference for moving abruptly between luminous images, a preference reflecting not only the impact of his early close reading of *The Pisan Cantos* but his first perceptions of the Italian landscape. After his discovery of Pound (a discovery of poetry as Pound, poetry as Italy, poetry as Italy-and-Pound) he attempted for two years "to rewrite" *The Cantos*.[28] His attempt is telling, evoking a neophyte's urge for imitation and his immense youthful confidence.

Surely his desire to retrace and reassess Pound as a poetic father must have been both dangerous and ideal. Dangerous because of Pound's fanatical ideology, his acknowledged megalomania, his late silences. And certainly Pound's forbidding edifice of knowledge and linguistic training must have seemed intimidating. And yet ideal, perhaps for precisely some of those same reasons: Pound not only offered an aesthetic method for emulation, a method that makes capacious use of allusion and language fragmentation, but his seemingly endless lacunae—part of the very fabric of *The Cantos*—presented an enabling strategy that amounted to an echo of Wright's imminent spiritual practices. In turn, Pound's aesthetic technique of assembling fragments, including diverse voices, is duplicated by Wright in his approach to self-identity as well as in his approach to the text; Wright avoids Pound's tragically corrupting political and social certainties by extending fragmentation to representations of his own personae. Doubt of authorial mastery plagues—and humbles—Wright. "Sometimes I erase so much I tear a hole in the paper" he notes in an interview in which he remarks on Pound's influence on his work.[29] His observation about his own vigorous erasing is recounted with both humor and pride, reflecting self-revision and continuing ambition. The act of tearing a hole in paper by erasing becomes analogous to an effect he seeks through words; he would break through a tissue of language and of materiality itself to suggest that which escapes language. He would insinuate that whatever resists material inscription resists critical accommodation.

In Wright's early poetry, Pound is cast as the "cold-blooded father of light." Like his Odysseus of *The Cantos*, Pound awaits his "voyage" into death, a voyage much like many that Wright will situate at his poems' borders:

> Here is your caul and caustic,
> Here is your garment,
> Cold-blooded father of light—
> Rise and be whole again.

(CM, 12)

Surely here is Wright's wish for the psychic resurrection of Pound, employed in the poem as a strategy of closure that works off the trope of ascension. Yet it is telling that the poem's symbolic natural forces speak against the desire of the speaker, for natural orders in the poem are undergoing disruption and dissolution, marking as such Wright's ambivalence.

Perhaps what attracted Wright to Pound was not only Pound's bold assemblage of materials and brisk movement without ligature between images, although Wright is more cohesive than Pound and limits his range of references, but his own perception of silence in Pound as much as speech. In "Improvisations on Pound," Wright narrates an anecdote that he heard from the critic David Kalstone. The anecdote may shed light on Wright's reasons for focusing so often on Pound as influence (Pound's name is tied to virtually all of Wright's self-accounts regarding his development as a poet):

> The only light seemed to gather on Pound's hands, he [Kalstone] said, everything else and everyone else in a kind of elusive, watery darkness, and throughout the time they sat there—while Pound apparently spoke, but inaudibly, his comments being repeated each time by Olga Rudge— Pound kept scratching at the back of one hand with the nails of the other, clawing almost, over and over, as though to rid himself of something: only the hands obsessively scratching in the artificial light, the voice inaudible and sibylline.[30]

In retelling Kalstone's story, Wright makes Pound a figure of the sibyl or prophet, failed but portentous. Pound is "inaudible," and yet his body confesses feeling, his gestures, perhaps at least in conventional terms, revealing a desire to purify or to "erase." Thus Wright gives Pound a curious ritualistic and divinatory status, a sort of aged unreality, as if the elder poet were the Sibyl of Cumae evoked in Eliot's epigraph to *The Waste Land*. Here Wright affords Pound the elaborate trappings of mysticism, trappings that seem more appropriate to Eliot than to Pound. (Eliot's issues—among them, the path between flesh and spirit and their point of possible meeting—are more clearly Wright's own than are Pound's historical and economic themes.) But perhaps it is the late Pound's silences and even his errors (Wright views *The Cantos* as "the most interesting failure of the century") that make him ultimately fascinating for Wright, and something of a renewable resource. Wright views Pound as a mysterious figure who cannot ultimately be known. Such a characterization is deeply attractive, for it echoes Wright's own conception of the elusive transcendent. And tracking the elusive transcendent has been the most generative pursuit for Wright as a poet. Indeed, Pound's practice of omission and Pound's status, for Wright, as an "omission" of sorts—an obscured figure of large gestures—are provocative. The elder poet's scope and ambition are certainly of great interest to Wright, who himself is ambitious and prolific, with a wide-ranging intelligence and a readerly sensibility. Of *The Cantos*, Wright observes, "[Pound] never finished the poem, it was abandoned"[31]—a statement that might reflect Wright's recognition of the inevitably uncompletable nature of his own project.

Beyond Pound, Wright's influences are numerous and he points to them readily. He has absorbed some of Dante and the influence of such figures as Hopkins, Yeats, Hart Crane, and Montale (whom he has translated) to the point that no one influence predominated even by his early midcareer. Complicating the issue of influence, Wright frequently has noted his affinity with Emily Dickinson, whom he makes rather an inhuman figure—somewhat as he does Pound. "One has to imagine that Emily Dickinson was inhabited. How else could she know those things?," he asks.[32] While Wright's tendency is to somewhat laboriously render Pound as a quasi mystic, Dickinson comes more conveniently as a nearly ready-made mystic of sorts. In a "Journal of the Year of the Ox" he describes his visit to the Dickinson mansion in Amherst, Massachusetts. In the poem, his persona looks through a window as he assumes Dickinson must have, noting details of weather and landscape, an isolated activity of observation that is familiar to us from many of Wright's poems. Although the speaker wishes that it would appear, the ghost of Dickinson does not make itself known. But the speaker registers an affection for the place where she lived, and he nearly ascertains a Dickinson-like presence until his name is called, apparently by his friends who have been waiting for him in the downstairs hallway. The quiet activities detailed in the poem are Wright's passions: intense observation and listening, a fruitless (but somehow nearly rapturous) waiting for a sign of sorts. As this scenario suggests, it may be as profitable an exercise to consider his affinities to Dickinson as to Pound, in that his poems, like Dickinson's, experiment with spiritual belief. Both Wright and Dickinson's metaphysical questions focus on much the same provisions, and both reveal an urge toward transcendence coupled with skepticism. His approach, similar to Dickinson's, is that of an investigatory doubter steeped in the language of religious ritual and yet passionate for the diurnal. Both poets are grounded in a keen sense of place and view paradox as endemic to language. For Wright, as his poems enclosing the figures of Pound or Dickinson suggest, any literary forebear is a compressed visual notation figured as a light source—a source of illumination within language. Each literary figure (for whom Pound and Dickinson serve as essential prototypes) is nevertheless finally "unreachable," a sort of departing light from which he might finally detect only faint traces of the otherworldly. With his "divines," literary or otherwise, any approximation of salvation lies in approach rather than in arrival, as in "Homage to Arthur Rimbaud":

> —Desperate to attempt
> An entrance, to touch that light
> which buoys you like a flame, . . .
>
> We cluster about your death
> As though it were reachable.
>
> (*CM*, 13)

Most often the summoned literary representative is already "risen" in this poetry, and literature is imaged as a possible means of ascension into a realm beyond suffering and loss. Yet the trope in this work is that of rising toward disappearance, an ascension out of sight, in a phosphorescent afterimage or afterpath. The literary figure is not only one who disappears but one who leaves behind in his or her poems emblems of absence.

In interviews and essays Wright is forthcoming about his aesthetic techniques. For Wright, the "odd marriage" of Dickinson and Whitman, the leisurely breadth of Whitman melded with the gnomic, imagistic units of Dickinson, must be conjoined.[33] His lines are built progressively, but each is meant to detain the reader, creating a discrete moment of intensity within the greater event of the poem. The line is most often speculative, pulling language forward into ever-widening conjectures. As such, the poet defeats the premature impulse toward closure:

> if one of the primary urges of a work of art is to become circular and come to a completion, then one of the real jobs of the artist is to keep the closure from happening so he can work in the synapse, the spark before the end.[34]

Such a forfeiture of "arrival," refusing a collapse into readily accessible meaning, echoes the deferred spiritual meetings that his speakers undergo. An imagistic openness, a renunciation of firm coloring-in and, often, of narrative continuity, is characteristic of his aesthetic. Similarly, his poems would be stripped of connectives, exfoliating gradually in a way that Wright has connected to his heritage as a Southerner: "A tendency toward the romantic, an identification with language as opposed to what we think of as nature, a desire to subtract rather than add, a liking for lushness in a spare context."[35]

It may be our impression of Wright's poems as emptying out or unfolding themselves, bearing wavering traces of meaning, that is peculiarly affecting. His change of style in the late 1970s occurs as a form of spatializing, an extension of the poem's boundaries as if they were the body's boundaries—as if even his self-representations would radiate outward eventually to occupy the place of his longed-for ideal. That is, the hide-and-seek with God enacted in so many of his poems is also a hide-and-seek with selfhood and identity, as reflected in the poems' spatial structures, which allow for delayed completion and "empty" white space. Wright structures his poems through definition by negation, undoing or reversing effects he has laboriously set up. He favors paradox and logical reversals ("I find myself in my own image, and am neither and both)" (*WTT,* 168), rhetorical devices that are prominent in both his prose and his poetry.

For Wright, a change in style reflects a change in the imagination of selfhood. In one of the most convincing arguments about Wright's poetry, James McCorkle calls Wright's work "an autobiography of energy and transmutation, where the self's writing collaborates with the natural world's writing."[36] With McCorkle's words in mind, it is instructive to compare Wright's emblematic natural images to those of Louise Glück. As we shall see in chapter 5, Glück, in her fifth book *The Wild Iris* (1992), gives voice to nature to represent human vulnerability and bafflement. Wright, in opposition, makes nature a voiceless accompaniment whose "actions"—the movement of foliage in wind, any natural response to seasonal change—resonate with his own philosophic musings. Wright composes the parable of the pepper tree or the oleander as nature's reflection of what the poems relentlessly state: destruction accompanies the appearance of order. Yet when symbols of nature counter a death instinct in the work, they do so only peripherally and momentarily. One of the curious effects of this work is that particulars of the natural world, however seemingly in close focus, dissipate amid the meditations that Wright outlines. Nature is beaded, worked over, and references to it are drawn from art, particularly from painting and music, as if Wright's nature is illustrated. He conveys physical relationship and movement in artful "unworldliness," moving the natural into the realms of art and the supernatural.

The Southern Cross (1981) retains its special status in Wright's work, embodying conflicting pressures most intensely. It is marked by traces of some of the blocklike imagistic density that he perfected in his previous four books. In addition, it reveals, with all the viscerality of discovery, an emerging aesthetic as he restructures his poems, particularly by loosening syntax and rhythms and extending line lengths. In *The Southern Cross* he infuses his poems with more casual moments than in his earlier books, creating a recognizable first person and narrative sequences that encompass a varied rhetorical range. The associations we bring to the book's title, conjuring not only the constellation but Wright's birthplace in Tennessee and his partial allegiance to a Southern Christian sensibility, announce that the astronomical and the salvific—and the torture of the cross—authorize the volume. But the book also allows us to make associations with the cross as a meeting point, and the cross as exit and bar, denying entry. The cross reflects his historical position, "crossed," in his metaphor, by the Episcopalianism of his youth, by a propensity for the Southern tall tale, and by a dearly acquired worldliness that threatens to cast spiritual belief as simple superstition.

The book opens with the eight-page paean "Homage to Paul Cézanne," composed as if to a ghost identity. The poem poses the questions: What can we do with the dead, and what can the dead do with us? The dead for Wright become an artistic medium, almost wholly aestheticized, just as the self for Wright turns into an artifact of writing. The dead are figured as paintlike or textual, revealing something to us of the future, as if writing were this poet's Ouija board with which he contacts the spirits of his own departed: "They point to their favorite words / Growing around them, revealed as themselves for the first time" (*WTT*, 4). The dead "dust over" nature with their dry essences and rise to request remembrance, even as Wright refers to them as artful materials, moving them into color, to "spread them," "layer them," "[c]ircle and smudge, cross-beak and buttonhook" them (*WTT*, 6). The dead in the opening section of *The Southern Cross* are aesthetic stand-ins; what they assume, the writer assumes:

> Like us, they refract themselves. Like us,
> They keep on saying the same thing, trying to get it right.
> Like us, the water unsettles their names.
>
> (*WTT*, 3)

However gently, the dead also camouflage and violate their living hosts. As Bruce Bond provocatively asserts of the poem, "Through the dead's eyes,

we are the transcendent." "Homage to Paul Cézanne" and many other of
Wright's poems aim to allow us to "see ourselves this way as well, made
expansive and unfamiliar in the world mirror."[37] This conceptual move
noted by Bond is fascinating; Wright would have us view ourselves as the
dead might: as suddenly strange, as "transcendent" in Bond's formulation—
a formulation that makes palpable the very uncanniness of the way this
poet inhabits and deploys language. As David St. John notes: "It is as if
many of Wright's poems keep seeking some ideogrammatic form"[38]—and
spatializing their arguments, it seems to me, by conveying the auditory quality
of poetry into the visual field.

  In "Tracing Charles Wright" Charles Bedient notes that for Wright
"revelation came early and has remained unsparing: it is that the dead,
who are superior to us, who know more and feel more, are always near
us."[39] Of Wright, Bedient says, "No one more medieval, more communal
in his relation to the dead."[40] Wright's position over time has become increasingly ambivalent, registering a desire for the presence of the dead and
nevertheless an obtrusive disbelief in regard to their presence. The self-
extinction that menaces his personae is mirrored in his fear of total extinction of not only physical life but spiritual intimations.

  "Homage to Paul Cézanne" prefaces a series of self-portraits in *The
Southern Cross* that further suggest, as we shall see, Wright's sense of lifeforms
as being inhabited by death. His self-portraits tend to emphasize mortality,
and they make the self "strange" to the self. His most focused renderings of
the self-portrait in *The Southern Cross* were preceded early in his career by
"Dog Creek Mainline" from *Hard Freight*, a poem that Wright credits with
teaching him the possibilities inherent in autobiographical poems. "Dog
Creek Mainline" opens with a visual and olfactory catalog. A sense of place
widens in memory and allows Wright to reenvision and requestion stages of
identity as the self is inevitably surrounded and defined by place. Places
take on bodily meaning, a blood knowledge, and each part of the body that
is mentioned in the poem—heart, ear, eye, and tongue—is mirrored in the
environment. Certainly the experience of writing the poem taught Wright
that autobiography could be flexibly cast through elements of landscape
that intimate spiritual desire in the abstract. The natural world is translated
for spiritual notation, and the self not only identifies with nature but is made
into an element of nature. In consequence, the self is not "confessed," not
personalized in daily action, but consecrated by the poet's observant sensibility ranging over his natural environment. In an interview, Wright cau-

tions about the factual references of his seemingly autobiographical poems: "[M]ost all of the stories that come out in my poems are things that not necessarily happened to me but I would like to have had happen to me."[41] For a poet so deeply—indeed, almost obsessively—attracted to transformation, he fears that the actual self may be stubbornly untransformative:

> It just suddenly occurred to me that there is a moment when what you are is what you're going to be. You will not be able to alter yourself. You have already made yourself into what you are. That time comes at different ages for everyone. Mine came in the fifth grade when I realized that I was the onlooker. . . . I was the person who was always doing the observing. This has continued in my life to this day.[42]

Despite his references to personal transformation in many of his poems, Wright suggests that there is no escape from the self. Certainly some of his poems attend to faith in a polyspiritual web of nature, even as his spiritual hunt for meaning erases conceptual origins; for Wright, reality seems to evade any vision of a founding moment or a central source of meaning. Yet he sees himself as a poet haunted by the limited, unconvertible, unchanging self, a self that relentlessly observes itself: "The past is the one mirror that never releases its images. Layer and overlay, year after year, wherever you look, however you look, whenever you look, it's always your own face you see there. All those years, and it's still your own face."[43]

Before *The Southern Cross* Wright had dealt with the autobiographical impulse almost systematically by centering on isolated incidents that defined key aspects of his past. In "Tattoos," from *Bloodlines*, events inscribed deeply upon his psyche are crystallized through images dense with implications. Such spiritualized and aestheticized blocks of memory deal with the death of his mother and father, religious ceremonies, and encounters in Italian cities. His ultimate objective in this series seems to be to project psychological condensations rather than psychological confessions. The series of twenty poems, largely cast in present tense, is ordered in a way that allows him to mark, to make an imprint upon, the language as he himself was deeply affected by each event. In such poems, the past is seductive but only illusorily capturable. At best it may be evoked, for instance, through a sequence of place names, and thus the self, which Wright fears may be limited and static, is rendered suggestively elusive.

Wright's desire to recall the past and to trace the outlines of a self is countered by another strain in his poems: he would unsettle a localized self, unmastering identity in language by writing toward the transcendent (just as God, whether approached through language, or landscape, is similarly "not in place"). His poems' instability, insisting that no one meaning be settled upon and refusing closure, would oppose the paralyzed and limited self. For Wright, while the same known face greets his in the mirror daily, ultimately self-representation is an impossibility of sorts—which may account, oddly enough, for his attraction to poems professing self-portraiture; he has always been a poet attracted to the impossible. Echoing Jorge Luis Borges, he writes by way of preface to *Country Music:*

> It has been suggested that all forms possess their virtue in themselves and not in any conjectural content. I don't entirely agree with this, but I do believe such a statement contains more truth than falsehood. It has also been suggested—again by Jorge Luis Borges—that everything a man writes, in the end, traces the outlines of his own face. I find it has been that way with me.[44]

Wright consciously aims toward a tracery of the self, an outline, rather than filled-in portraiture, as if "Form tends toward its own dissolution" (*WTT,* 208), including the dissolution of the autobiographical center.

Given his fondness for peripheral and fleeting images and his preference for abbreviated anecdotes about the self, it is perhaps surprising that few contemporary poets have placed the self-portrait under such sustained and yet ironic focus. "The poem is a self-portrait / always, no matter what mask / You take off and put back on" (*WTT,* 97). If every poem is a self-portrait, poems actually titled self-portraits reflexively point to lyric selfhood as plural and shifting, and capable of continual reframing. In another context he refers to autobiography as "a kind of minus tide that runs just under everything and adds by subtraction."[45] He has proven attentive to the project of presenting a self not only aware of mortality but given to the rehearsal of its own death—as if to dislodge threatening conceptions of an overly defined, limited self, harnessed by its recognizable social identity. Notably, the lyric poet is a "self-traitor" to one voice; the lyric self must "smuggle in" devices that affront simplicity (*WTT,* 21). The self-portrait by Wright enacts an identification between self and language: the self's insufficiencies and the language's, yes, but also the proliferating energy of language that may be discovered by contemplating selfhood.

In his midcareer Wright draws increasing attention to the lyrical first person, self-referentially language-made, for he recognizes poetry as his integral route of knowing. Poetry "is the one boat . . . that's going to get me across the river," he told Elizabeth McBride.[46] He remains less distrustful of images cast in language than enamored of the multiplicity of meaning that they make possible. He asks for "A little vowel for the future, a signal from us to them" (*WTT,* 18). In another turn, "Language can do just so much, / a flurry of prayers, / A chatter of glass beside the road's edge, / Flash and a half-glint as the headlights pass" (*WTT,* 20). In such tropes, language is likened to the scene of an accident; words appears to us in sudden, brief, and puzzlingly partial illuminations. Nevertheless, this "just so much" remains a great deal, for the ephemerality of effects, the referential slide of language, its "flurry," "chatter," and "flash," become the motions he chooses most consistently to describe, the visual incidents that he finds most appealing and that most closely approximate his experience of being.

Five forays into a way of saying "I" in the second section of *The Southern Cross* suggest that Wright hopes to make the first-person pronoun excessive, transcending physical and cultural limits. For this poet, the language of poetry is a way of both making and unmaking selfhood, a means of singing selves into and out of being, of assembling bits of memory and abandoning preconceptions about their meaning. His five fifteen-line poems titled "Self-Portrait" in *The Southern Cross* attempt to make the self estranged to the self through repetition; that is, like a familiar word that has been repeated until it seems odd to us, the self-portraits in this series attempt a defamiliarizing perspective. That the poems are interrupted by longer, more anecdotal pieces further intensifies our awareness of discontinuous identities. Wright offers his characteristic devices of self-examination—lists of places, photographs, landscapes, prayers, and lyric poets—to move toward a self inhabited by "the ghost-weight" of the once-forgotten dead. He reemphasizes the nature of language as his ostensible subject, for the portrait in words becomes a portrait of words.

Wright's first self-portrait in *The Southern Cross* prefigures his last in formulating a prayer of deliverance from a simple stable self in favor of a self capable of enlarging its sympathy. In Wright's series the self would be a fugitive from certainty, about to be "rearranged":

> From the mulch and the undergrowth, protect me and pass
> me on.
> From my own words and my certainties,
> From the rose and the easy cheek, deliver me, pass me on.

The first portrait is unremittingly self-focused; its speaker, being "found out," will "hum to [him]self," meditating on the present moment, the passivity of plants, and the place he occupies. But this contemplation of nature is interrupted by Wright's characteristic prayerlike plea: a petition against self-complacency, against the sort of vegetal passivities that lie in wait for him, against, that is, what seem to be his instincts for preserving his own ego. "The ashes and bits of char that will clear my name" (*WTT,* 11) not only suggest the extinction of identity in death, but insinuate that death is a release from the limitation of being and from an initially unspecified sin. This unnamed sin seems, in context, to be that of complacency, indifference, and self-satisfaction. Wright thus opens the series by expressing the hope to be "unfixed" and absolved of blame.

In the second self-portrait the self and textuality are united, yet being and writing make absence curiously almost tangible. Investigating the self as if it were a text, Wright looks with detachment at this "Charles," this "infinite alphabet of his past." "The wind will edit him soon enough," he predicts of his "earmarked" persona. His speaker, "Holding the pages of a thrown-away book" (*WTT,* 13), is ever aware of his own transience as a creature of words and redaction, and he would seem to fade into his own text.

From verbal images, Wright moves on to photographic images. His third self-portrait reflects "camera range" in images of Wright's father and brother. Of course, the future of the photographer's subjects is known by the one holding the photograph. And in this small act of holding the photograph and knowing the fate of its subjects, it is possible for the speaker to feel (at least momentarily) almost a God-like foreknowledge. Wright sharpens the irony of assuming such inflated knowledge by insisting on ignorance of his own future. Static representations are "evidence" that Wright regards only as suggestive pointers:

> Checking the evidence, the postcards and the photographs,
> O'Grady's finger pointing me out . . .
>
> Madonna of Tenderness, Lady of Feints and Xs, you point too.
>
> (*WTT,* 16)

He juxtaposes the human specificity of O'Grady with the otherworldly divines of woe and ephemeral effects. Two pointings, O'Grady's and the Madonna of Tenderness's, earthly and otherworldly, must be engaged if life and death, earth and spirit, are to form a more complete iconography.

Furthering his investigation, the fourth self-portrait calls up lyric poets of the past. Whitman is engaged at the poem's start, along with a list of places and dead literary figures. This self-portrait makes memory elastic, moving back in time by two decades and projecting a self as dust and evaporate, a ghostlier self than has so far appeared in his self-portrait series. At the poem's conclusion, Wright supplicates a literary pantheon: "Dino Campana, Arthur Rimbaud. / Hart Crane and Emily Dickinson. The Black Château" (*WTT,* 19). While we think of catalogs as most frequently centering on presence, Wright introduces his own sequence of names of dead literary figures to point up spiritual absences.

Each of the self-portraits in *The Southern Cross* that we have discussed provides an account that is explicitly partial, preparing for and augmenting the fifth self-portrait as it extends from a localized persona's early past toward communal impulse. What begins as the most rooted of portraits and the most straightforward in syntax moves toward the language of communal need. In the final portrait in this series, Wright depicts a spiritual presence as an "undoer and rearranger." Moreover, this persona is further inhabited, "the ghost-weight of a past life in my arms, / A life not mine." The self is inhabited by the dead, here a feminine imploring figure of ill fortune. This counterself, an interior ghost, is herself engaged in Wright's characteristic pose of expectancy, "still waiting to rise." The speaker's self is permeable, inhabited by the dead and by the "evening [that] becomes us." The dead figure seems like a lover, yet Wright wishes for a note of commonality toward the living: "Hold hands, hold hands / That when the birds start, none of us is missing. / Hold hands, hold hands" (*WTT,* 21). The series ends as a lyric evocation for contact before absolute loss. The final cry, "hold hands," enacts a new patterning; to hold hands is to make a physical human design. The lyric "I" comes closer to a "we," a communal singing.

According to Northrop Frye, "The lyric is the genre in which the poet, like the ironic writer, turns his back on his audience."[47] Wright seems to have had his back to readers in this series of self-portraits, and yet finally and surprisingly moves away from the solitary meditative mode to create the illusion of emerging before an audience. Breaking out of his meditation, he suddenly assumes communion with the invitation "Hold hands."

What, then, is the self-portrait for Wright? Representations of selfhood become ways of questioning traditional means of saying "I" and assuming social identity by insisting on nonbeing, a "ghost-weight," the perception of immateriality in selfhood. The lyric poet is like that personage whom the poet calls "the spider love," an "undoer and rearranger," making a network of presence and absence. Inevitably no self-portrait is adequate, for the project of representing an ultimate integral self in language must elude us. To compose such a self-portrait in words is eventually to make a cry not only outward toward a gallery of spiritual guides but finally, however tentatively, to a human community united by awareness of death. The "I" emerges as a simile of sorts, a bridge toward other presences, those ghosts of nonbeing as well as those O'Gradys of the flesh. As Wright suggests, "The 'I' persona that I often use in my poems is not, I hope, the 'merely personal' I of so many poems that one sees. I hope it does go through a kind of sea-change into the richness of the impersonal, where the true and touchable personal actually lives."[48]

Throughout a poetry that examines the lyric first person as a precarious text of sorts, Wright enacts his awareness of the difficulty for the contemporary poet who writes in the first person. That he does so has been an occasion for discomfort for some critics, a discomfort that X. J. Kennedy voiced in reviewing Wright: "He is serious, unafraid, and a master of intelligent music. Perhaps theme, and Tennessee, will yet weight him and steady him down."[49] Kennedy's is an eloquent wish, but one that ignores Wright's essential project, which disavows a "weighted" self or central wholeness in favor of selves that move between extremes. Wright prefers to flicker imagistically between Tennessee and Italy, the natural and the artificial, rising and falling, the living and the dead, rather than to alight and "steady" himself. For Wright, to make a self-portrait in "a language where nothing stays" is to ride, however disconcertingly, upon a wavelike knowledge of appearance and disappearance.

That Wright's self-portrait series finally broadens, even if briefly, toward the suggestion of communal chant suggests the permeability of his lyric selves as well as a recognition of his audience. "No one is listening," Wright concludes section 9 of an early series of poems. That someone now might indeed be listening Wright seems to presume within the more intimate tone of his work after *China Trace*. Helen Vendler, writing of his early work, describes Wright's as "the poetry of the transcendent 'I' in revolt against the too easily articulate 'I' of social engagement and social roles. Whether one 'I' can address his word to other hidden 'I's' across the abyss of daily life without using the personal, transient, and social language of that life is the question Wright poses."[50] In work after the late 1970s, however, he presents the self less as the transcendent "I" and more as an "I" willing to rehearse death even while scaling various ranges of selfhood. The recording of transience has clearly become his project. He acknowledges a way of writing selves into and out of being, crossing gaps, executing self-portraits as testing measures of identity. "It's synaptical here, / And rearranged" (*WTT*, 114), he tells us of his poems, in which abandonments and disappearances are cast in a vocabulary of ascents and descents. This lyric mode liquefies boundaries between past and present and being and nonbeing. The first-person inconclusive, a "traitor" to simple identity, becomes the first-person plural in Wright. Posing both evaporations and new gatherings, these self-portraits would allow us to imagine the projected loss of any singular identity, as Wright reimagines selfhood as unfinished and "lavish."

Wright further defines his position in "Gate City Breakdown," a poem unusual for Wright, for it is more openly conversational, less narratively "rearranged" than many of his lyrics of the same period. His speaker describes speeding in a car with other Tennessee boys. As a self-portrait, the poem makes certain claims on us even while seeming to efface its speaker:

> Jesus, it's so ridiculous, and full of self-love,
> The way we remember ourselves,
>   and the dust we leave . . .
>
> Remember me as you will, but remember me once
> Slide-wheeling around the curves,
>   letting it out on the other side of
>   the line.
>   (*WTT*, 40)

By "letting it out on the other side of the line," Wright focuses in the vernacular on his fluency with the line break (he is surely one of our contemporary masters) and, more important, suggests that he would present himself as a poet escaping the universal sheriff of law and order, running his aesthetic "moonshine" across the borders of poetic convention.

The prominence of vertical motion throughout Wright's work bears further on this issue of establishing and dissolving private selfhood and public identity through language. Wright charts a self in continual motion or in irreal suspension between dramatic alternatives. Ascending, descending, rising, falling: these participles appear frequently in Wright's work, early and late. It seems clear that his focus on descent is not simply a conventional metaphor for the human fall from a realm of grace; the fall he writes of depicts being itself as dynamically moving toward nonbeing.

In *The Other Side of the River* (1984), Wright adopts a more leisurely inclusion of anecdotes than in his previous poetry, particularly anecdotes of near falls that echo the highly charged patterns of imagery throughout his work. He narrates incidents of suspension or descent in which survival appears contingent. In "Lonesome Pine Special," for instance, the persona's car has "spun out" with "one front wheel on a rock, / and the other on air, / Hundreds of feet down the mountainside" (*WTT,* 72). The speaker must balance there, close to extinction. Similarly, in "Italian Days" a helicopter engine has stopped "And we began to slide sideways down the air, / As quietly as a snowflake" (*WTT,* 87). The irreality of the moment, its strange delicacy and silence, duplicates in narrative form Wright's conceptual emphasis upon the provisional nature of selfhood: if there are many representations of selves that Wright longs to deploy in language, none of them are less liable to extinction. In "Two Stories" (*WTT,* 75–77) Wright tells first of his speaker as a boy camper who has sleepwalked to the edge of a drop-off and wakes to face both the drop-off and a bear. The child is granted a miraculous reprieve and returns to his tent unscathed. In the second story, a rattlesnake, several hours dead, bruises a man's wrist; the "stump" of the snake strikes. Similar to tall tales, such narratives illustrate the closeness of death to the living in ways that Wright has always presented imagistically in his work. Rather than a departure, the frequent inclusion of such anecdotes in *The Other Side of the River* underscores his characteristic concern with unusual physical and psychic states.

As Wright has it, his work becomes "this business I waste my heart on. / / And nothing stops that" (*WTT,* 38); the desire to make poems, making selves out of language, comes closest to certainty for him. Wright is clearly a poet who cannot entertain complacency and punishes himself if he lapses even momentarily into any relaxation of his aesthetic and spiritual pursuits. As a number of his readers have noted, his poetry is characterized by melancholy rather than anger, a tonal quality that is alien to the zeal of much neosurrealist practice and that depends upon confessionalism's legacy of ruthless self-examination. "Whatever it is, it bothers me all the time" is Wright's refrain, uttered three times in the five-line stanzas of "Laguna Blues," progressing from the riddle in the mind, to the riddle in the song/ poem, to whatever's "off-key and unkind" (*WTT,* 23). The refrain might be his signature piece with its light humor and its conceptual repetition. "Whatever it is," "the unknown and unknowable" does not leave him alone.

While Wright's dilemma initially may seem ahistorical, it is, in greater measure, a cultural and even a generational one. As Norman Finkelstein notes: "The absence of the sublime may offer relief to many 'radical' Postmodernists, who perceive the sublime as nothing more than an exhausted mode of bourgeois literary discourse, but its absence provides a devastating tension for these poets who experience it first-hand."[51] Julia Kristeva, for one, speculates about the inescapability of melancholy for any creative imagination: "[T]here is no imagination that is not, overtly or secretly, melancholy."[52] Wright surely would seem to express an intensification of his generation's melancholy. Both Bedient and Pinsky note such a strain in Wright. Bedient observes: "A jubilant melancholic, this poet—like every poet—leads a second life (it may feel like the only one) of figures, rhythms, and meanings, exalted and artificial, eloquent and to-be-continued."[53] Bedient further draws upon Susan Sontag's speculations about Walter Benjamin's melancholia to support his assertion about Wright as melancholic: "'He has complex, often veiled relations with others.' Other Saturnine traits—among them the view of time as a 'medium of constraint, inadequacy, repetition,' the compulsion 'to convert time into space,' indecisiveness, a 'self-conscious and unforgiving relation to the self'—are conspicuous in Wright's work."[54] Robert Pinsky notes the same propensity in depicting Wright's sensibility as melancholic: "It is as though the constant, unrelaxing stream of dense poetic language is the only way to relieve the painful memories and bad foreboding which are Wright's characteristic materials."[55]

Wright's poetry grows perhaps increasingly melancholic in its regard for contemporary culture. In their ruminations, Wright's poems bear the mark of his resistance to much of contemporary Western culture and its superficial innovation and frenetic consumerism. The poems insist on the ephemerality of the material (even as Wright casts affectionate attention on nature, he shades natural phenomena with references to silence and absence) and bespeak an oppositional cultural position in late-twentieth-century America. Moreover, the poems reflect a difference from culture in their melancholy near ennui, their desire to purify their speakers of egoism, their antimaterialism, and even their refusal of haste. He would oppose other contemporary conditions, including a climate of therapeutic cheer and a wholesale cultural embrace of technological innovation that encourages heterogeneous but shallow desires.

Perhaps it is not surprising, then, that visions of contemporary apocalypse are close to this poet, a fact that the poems confront in outward rhetoric and disparate images. In the final poem of *The Other Side of the River* Wright presents one of his more devastating indictments of a future. His

landscape in "California Dreaming" glitters with the ultimate destruction
of any vestige of self or selves. We have not arrived at the other side of the
river but rather at Lethe and a surrounding landscape of Darvon and Valium.
He creates a particularized environment in which the inner life has been
reduced as his speaker finds himself adrift in a testing ground: a California
of sorts that seems be a state of spiritual inertia. The poem details anesthe-
tized self-unraveling, beginning with the projected extinction of both identity
and world, all orchestrated to a superficially inconsequential voice hum-
ming a popular song:

> Piece by small piece the world falls away from us like
>   spores
> From a milkweed pod,
>   and everything we have known,
> And everyone we have known,
> Is taken away by the wind to forgetfulness,
> Somebody always humming,
>   California dreaming . . .
>   (*WTT,* 118)

Calypsoed in this strange California of the soul, Wright chooses earlier in
the poem to send out a chain of similes by which to travel:

> What I know best is a little thing.
> It sits on the far side of the simile,
>   the like that's like the like.
>   (*WTT,* 116)

He must look warily for signs of immanence, attending with concentrated
discipline to his environment.

"For over a half century I've waited in vain" (*WTT,* 229), Wright notes
elsewhere. His poems are willfully repetitious as if they are what he has
called the "worry beads" of a man who has abandoned a prescribed faith.
Just the same, it would be a mistake to think of his notations as acknowledgments of defeat. However abandoned by his divinity, or absolute meaning,
it is the melancholy art of tense expectation that sustains this poetry into a
future.

Almost never lost in these poems is the depiction of a first person as a
realm of desires, desires to discover the next poem in "a language where
nothing stays" (*WTT,* 33). In Wright's returns to Italy, to Laguna Beach, to

the landscapes of his Southern childhood, to the inner life of quiet contemplation, he would call up a necessary language. While this attentive pursuit in language is akin to belief, it is a belief that cannot wholly suffice—and thus prompts Wright to compose the next poem as a means for discovering the elusive epiphany.

The title of Wright's eleventh book, *Chickamauga*, refers to the battlefield where the poet's great-grandfather and namesake, a Confederate captain, was shot in the mouth. After the battle of Chickamauga, Wright's great-grandfather was captured and for two years confined at Rock Island. "And came back to Little Rock and *began his career*." He was dead at sixty-six, "a ticket to Cuba stored flat in his jacket pocket" (*WTT,* 106). The story of Wright's great-grandfather is not only that of a mouth wound (with all the resonance such a wound evokes for a poet) but also a narrative of restlessness and action in the public world. The name of the battlefield in which Wright's forebear fought is thus talismanic, suggesting Wright's own psychic battlefield.

The book's first section is titled "Aftermath," directing attention to Wright's interest in exploring endings and outcomes. At the same time, the section title plays on assessing life as a form of mathematics, alluding to Wright's customary search for "equations" of meaning. "Sitting Outside at the End of Autumn" rehearses a number of Wright's characteristic gestures by relating his earnest effort to create, even to force, meaning from the daily particulars of his life. He centers on the landscape as a way to apprehend an innerspace or soulscape. In this, the first poem of *Chickamauga*, Wright expresses immediate failure; his grand project of determining autobiographical meaning has not been fulfilled. In the autumn of later middle age the speaker thumbs a snail shell. "I rub it clockwise and counterclockwise, hoping for anything / Resplendent in its vocabulary or disguise." He refers to Lao Tzu to pose a conundrum, to make a figure, "looking to calculate" his life's meaning.[56]

As his final poem in the collection, "Yard Work," indicates, the poet's business is to measure space and time through deployment of the line on the page and, by extension, to measure his own spiritual and aesthetic nature within the actual physical space that nature affords him. "My job is yard work— / I take this inchworm, for instance, and move it from here to there" (*C,* 92). As the poem suggests, in his quiet way Wright is a poet of puns, confident in using the terms of our grammar—the sentence, the line, the measure—to disport on nature, ethics, and, self-reflexively, his own poetic. "The invisible" and "the absolute," referred to individually in the first

and second stanza of the poem, are brought together in the third stanza as
if to emphasize that Wright's aesthetic is founded on a virtual mill of words.

Ultimately in this collection Wright would ask that the limits of the self
and its reliance on a publicly sanctioned identity be abandoned, as in "Looking Across Laguna Canyon at Dusk, West-by-Northwest":

> Like others, I want to pour myself into the veins of the
>   invisible
> at times like this,
>   becoming all that's liquid and moist.
> Like Dionysus, I'd enter the atmosphere,
>   spread and abandon—. . . .
>
> (C, 88)

This poem insinuates that the self made of words enacts its own disappearance in Wright's poems of his later career. Even more than wishing for
presence, such poems further rehearse an abandonment of identity, an active self-annihilation, a paean to invisibilities as the poet yearns for a loss of
secure identity boundaries. Through such an imagined merging with nature and godhead, Wright desires and verges on, but never quite entirely
allows for, ecstatic self-abandon. His portraits of spiritualized desires give
us, as Wright has said, the "outline" of a face. In an age of ever more heated
confessions in mass communications, he announces and defends obscure
sensations allied to the private even as the private in his poetry turns out to
be made of ethers and implosions.

In "Lives of the Saints," in *Black Zodiac*, Wright contemplates two of his
key themes: mortality and the yearning for God. Amid reminders of contemporary despair and violence in the poem—pimps and prostitutes and drive-
by shootings—he pronounces his own wariness as a "lookout and listener."[57]
Yet his evocation of Zen at the poem's close carries little conviction:

> Contemplative, cloistered, tongue-tied,
>   Zen says, watch your front.
> Zen says, wherever you are is a monastery.

It is the final two lines that utter a deeper resolve: "The lives of the saints
become our lives. / God says, watch your back."[58]

"Lives of the Saints" laments the failure to arrive at "the new and nego-
tiable, / The undiscovered snapshot"[59] even as the middle-aged poet pon-

ders his life's work as evasive substance over style, as, that is, elusive religious transformation: "We believe in belief but don't believe, / for which we shall be judged."[60] His skepticism, inevitably, keeps him from too easily assuming an oracular mantle. Wright has stated that his poems resemble "prayers," but more often one sees the poems as what he calls "unanswered prayers." They are framed repeatedly as if Wright can hardly help himself; he cannot avoid, that is, locating his aesthetic in the terms of spiritual feeling in which, like a saint, he too emerges for his readers as iconic, his essence unknowable.

Despite the bulking threat of mortality, Wright commends disciplined yearning for the divine and perpetual aesthetic alertness even as he suffers toward an assumption of belief. Such habits, characteristic of "the lives of the saints," become less a mark of individual distinction than of what he sees as a common path. To watch one's back, as he tells us God advises, is to watch for death and loss, an attentiveness that Wright seemed predisposed toward from early in his career. "Happiness happens, like sainthood, in spite of ourselves" (*WTT,* 193), he acknowledges. But, then, giving the lie to our hopes of settling upon and reaching our desires, in another poem he remarks: "Sadness is truer than happiness" (*WTT,* 141).

2

Cruel Figures:
The "Anti-Forms" of Russell Edson

Russell Edson returns us to an early meaning of *abandon*; that is, his characters are proscribed arbitrarily, for they are "under the jurisdiction of" forces within language and culture that they cannot examine freely. They are plagued by their inability to analyze language structures. His characters experience few impulsions other than a drive for predictability that forbids any living change or appropriate response to suffering. Edson concentrates on human deprivations, and while he might initially seem to be creating ahistorical fabular constructs, his concerns ultimately are ethical and reflect his cultural situation. Almost without exception no solution can be imported into the closed boundaries of his writing; no epiphany of any substance allows his characters insight into their situations. In his alternately stern and hilarious prose poems, Edson reveals himself to be preoccupied with the horrors human beings visit upon one another.

His most often repeated stylistic features include rapid speech exchanges between characters, a literalizing of metaphors, an identification of characters as types (Father, Mother, Old Man, Old Woman), definition by negation, and repetitions of language patterns that reflect his poems' forbidden content until unconscious associations spring upon the reader. He plots highly kinesthetic yet depthless scenes for his creatures intent on self-destruction or destruction of others. Indeed, in Edson's works, Henri Bergson's definition of humor, "something mechanical encrusted on the living," becomes more on the order of "something living encrusted on the mechanical." The juggernaut of will, possession, and ultimate mechanization overtakes all being.

It is a critical commonplace to note that in Edson's prose poems, humans, animals, and objects interpenetrate. A raincoat performs an autopsy;

a woman gives birth to a toad from her armpit; a man has sexual inter-course with a bicycle; a group of Americans are transformed into fish; a man dresses a cow in a wedding gown and a chicken in a smoking jacket; airplanes copulate and reproduce; chairs have a point of view. Such trans-formations hardly could be signs of a resonant or saving fluidity. People and objects are transformed only to make more clear the ironclad psychic pe-rimeters that they inhabit. The empowered act all the more viciously upon the unempowered who have been newly transformed, and any character's attempt to achieve meaningful self-integration or self-sovereignty fails mis-erably. Things may consciously conform to or subvert human will. As Donald Hardy points out, "Edson's critique of rationalism includes not only spoofs on basic human activities such as eating, but also attacks on all attempts to define the individual human as unique and separate from both the remain-der of the animal world, including other humans, and the inanimate world—especially the attempts to do so in science, history, art, and philosophy."[1] In this realm, Edson echoes André Breton, who in "On Surrealism in Its Liv-ing Works" argues that surrealism "does not lead . . . to its sharing in any way the opinion that man enjoys absolute superiority over all other beings, or, put another way, that man is the world's crowning achievement—which is the most unjustifiable sort of postulate and the most arrant abuse that anthromorphism [*sic*] can be charged with."[2]

Edson discovered his themes early in his career and has held to them. He lays cruelty bare by portraying objectification of living being as the concrete result of cultural ideologies. The primary relation between hu-man beings in his prose poems is coercive. As Denise Levertov has ob-served, Edson writes a prose poetry that makes cruelty manifest. "He is able to pass without loss of grace from the hilarious to a kind of dark gothick beauty, and sometimes to a tenderness that reveals him as no cruel puppetmaster but the anguished beholder of inexplicable cruelties."[3] For all their seeming absurdity, his prose poems are shaded by moral feeling, particularly by his disgust toward patterns of ideological violence. In his prose poems human agency is frustrated by predetermined forms. Even a notion of the private self is abandoned in favor of an ultimate objectification of being and experience. With particular vividness he portrays the absence of any appropriate affective response to suffering. That is, his characters' fail-ure to recognize and to respond thoughtfully to brutality, both to their own brutality and to that of others, accounts for much of his prose poems' unset-tling capacities.

Without recognition of pain, Edson suggests, there can be no recognition of significant consequences. His vision of late-twentieth-century culture calls for representations of the functionalizing and denial of suffering not only of others but of the very self that suffers or observes suffering. His characters, in their lack of affect or in their sudden outbursts (proliferating screams, for example), defeat claims to reason. As T. W. Adorno observed, suffering subverts our reason: "[R]ational cognition has one critical limit which is its inability to cope with suffering. Reason can subsume suffering under concepts; it can furnish means to alleviate suffering; but it can never express suffering in the medium of experience, for to do so would be irrational by reason's own standards."[4] Edson's ability to purvey "irrationality" depends on our noticing what is missing in his characters' responses; that is, it depends on what is not "reasonable" about their reactions to suffering.

In Edson's prose poetry, structures—whether of hierarchical social arrangement, gender, or language as mastering and pervasive form—tragically constrict and deplete human agency. His prose poems reflect the order of culturally sustained ideologies that are structured through violence. Indeed, the title of *The Very Thing That Happens* (1964), the collection that first brought him critical attention, may be literalized. His characters' deadpan acceptance of whatever initially appears to be perverse and improbable in their environments reflects Edson's focus on political "actuality," that is, on *the very thing that happens*. Lack of affect among his characters reflects his sense that the events they undergo are psychological correlatives and entirely predictable outcomes of what he sees as his culture's obsession with violence. While praised for his "enormous expressive freedom,"[5] Edson reveals checks on expression, particularly in his examinations of accepted structures of thought. Although the content of his prose poems seems utterly unpredictable, their focus, on one level, is upon what is absolutely predictable: the seemingly unassailable forms and formulae of linguistic and cultural convention.

In his work from 1960 to the present, Edson makes visible the saturation of the private with ideologies that promote violence and render it inevitable. His prose poems investigate an unconscious logic that structures demonstrations of oppressive power. Unfortunately, Edson's prose poems have often been viewed as ahistorical manifestations of the primitive energies of the id. As if they were free-floating anomalies, his prose poems are sometimes considered perversely resistant to explanation. Denise Levertov argues, "His art—its syntax, its elegant dryness, its bizarre condensed events—is the unique outgrowth of an eccentric imagination, the convoluted shell of the mind's hypersensitive, clairvoyant snail."[6] In one of the more quizzical characterizations of Edson's work, Robert Bly has contended that Edson writes the poetry that a chicken might. Bly's formulation is invoked in an article in the *American Poetry Review* by Donald Hall, who argues that "[f]ew people have *ever* written as Edson does, out of a whole irrational universe—infantile, paranoiac—with its own small curved space complete to itself, impenetrable by other conditions of thought."[7] Although no consensus about the prose poems' meanings has developed, surely suggestions that they are "impenetrable by other conditions of thought" prematurely limit our readings. In fact, I wish here to argue that Edson's prose poems are profoundly political, questioning forms of power summoned in language. They are not aesthetically boxed curiosities or a minimalist's freak show. Instead, like rather remarkable mirrors, they reflect the psychic consequences of social and cultural behaviors. Without domesticating his work as a prose poetry of simple ideological effects, I hope to demonstrate that Edson illuminates unconscious structures that inform public and private politics. Rather than ahistorical fables seemingly uncontaminated by contemporary culture, his prose poems are a darkly comic manifestation of culture.

The other poets discussed in this book have written prose poems, but none has done so with Edson's sustained concentration or aesthetic and ideological self-consciousness. By choosing the prose poem as his primary genre for imaginative composition, Edson not only reveals his uneasiness with predetermined literary form but capitalizes upon it, for the prose poem is a hybrid that resists definition. As Mary Ann Caws observes: "Having no necessary exterior framework, no meter or essential form, [the prose poem] must organize itself from within."[8] A genre that overlaps literary boundaries, the prose poem seems particularly well suited to aesthetic experimentation, revealing "multiple perspectives, changeable limits, floating borders and shifting contours."[9] The prose poem's union of both prose and poetry's stylistic conventions makes it attractive to writers intent on defeating generic expectations. And its generic uncanniness reflects a view of the real and actual as irreducibly strange.

Edson repeatedly has argued against the perception of the prose poem as a "form." As practiced by Edson, the prose poem registers a revolt against traditional aesthetic structures. "In one sense it might be seen as an antiform," Edson argues.[10] He would initiate a process of writing away from literature-as-he-has-known-it, as he asserts in "The Prose Poem in America":

> The writer coming to the prose poem has no rules to keep, and just as importantly, no rules to break. For in spite of all the poets who have written prose poems no aesthetic or compositional tradition has formed around the prose poem. I see this as one of its virtues. It is still the property of whoever is writing them.[11]

Edson observes, in fact, that "it is only incidental that [prose poems] are written out; the spirit or approach which is represented in the prose poem is not specifically literary."[12] Of course all things, including prose poems, possess "shape." But the prose poem avoids preconceived literary shape as it fills with "the psychic material that longs to be substance."[13] He is particularly anxious to overturn conceptions of the prose poem as reliant on earlier models, and he diminishes or dismisses much of the prose poem's literary lineage. As such, he is suspicious of the critical propensity to track the prose poem back through progenitors: "I don't think a line of European virtuosos is necessary to find the availability of the prose poem in America."[14] His position may remind us of Jean-François Lyotard's explication of James Joyce's development as a writer: "The grammar and vocabulary of literary language are no longer accepted as given; rather, they appear as academic forms, as rituals originating in piety (as Nietzsche said) which prevent the unpresentable from being put forward."[15] For Edson, prose poems emerge most fully from what is seemingly "unpresentable" in psychological compulsion; that is, the desire to make prose poems, in Edson's terms, arises from psychological need rather than emulation of the known: "One comes to the writing table with one's own hidden life . . . not dragging Pound's *Cantos*."[16] The prose poem may not be simply defined by originary conventions, literary, social, or otherwise, but reveals the structure of those very conventions, magnifying them so that they may at last become visible to those of us who are too readily accustomed to and accepting of cultural constructions.[17]

Edson displays a compulsion to expose base desires and fears. Although he came to maturity at a point when the New Critics maintained sway in colleges and universities, he sees the prose poem as resonant process rather than as aesthetic object. He displays an unambiguous commitment to writing as it reveals instinctive drives, on the one hand gleefully disclosing aggression and, on the other hand, as I have noted, insinuating in many poems a contained rage at human cruelty. Whether he sees his prose poems as anti-forms or half-finished forms—quasi definitions that he has applied at various times—he avoids producing complete categorizations.

Edson designed, set by hand, and printed his first collection, *A Stone is Nobody's*, in 1961, a year when the prose poem, familiar in Europe, had only begun to claim practitioners or critical interest in North America. Michael Benedikt argues that until the 1960s "no poetry remained quite as isolated from central international literary currents" as poetry in the United States.[18] He indicates that T. S. Eliot's largely "English-based, antinternationalist critical approach"[19] successfully blocked Anglo-American attention to continental poetry, thus inhibiting attention to prose poetry, with its formal roots in France in the writing of Charles Baudelaire. In his 1976 introduction, Benedikt argues that when Eliot's critical influence waned in the early 1960s, a poetry more open to international influences began to develop in the United States—a poetry written by poets responsive, in turn, to greater freedom of genre. In Benedikt's analysis, not only does the prose poem's highly charged employment of poetic resources combined with its absence of lineation define the genre, but the prose poem's reliance on unconscious processes proves a primary characteristic: "This attention to the unconscious, and to its particular logic, unfettered by the relatively formalistic interruptions of the line break, remains the most immediately apparent property of the prose poem."[20]

Jonathan Monroe focuses in greater depth upon the prose poem's international development in political terms: "[T]he failure of bourgeois society radically to alter its own forms of organization yields to experimentation with a genre that has as its project the undermining of received literary and extraliterary discursive practices." Monroe notes that the prose poem formally emerged in nineteenth-century France in conjunction with political unrest. It follows, he argues, that prose poetry would at last gain significant numbers of practitioners in the United States during the political dissent of the late 1960s.[21]

As one of the first poets of his generation in North America to exploit the prose poem, and as one of the relatively few writers in the United States successfully to have gained a reputation for working predominantly in the genre, Edson views the prose poem as a necessary means for writerly freedom—a freedom that he describes in terms of dreams. "This kind of creating should have as much ambition as a dream, which I assume most of us look upon, meaning our nightly dreams, as throwaway creations, not things to be collected in a book of poems."[22] Prose poems exhibit a dreamlike quality in which logical categories are violated or reversed. At the same time, his writing-as-dream-work is a destructive discipline, one of his prose poems suggests: "One has only to see the typewriter as the console of a kind of dream organ which, when played toward ecstasy, must bring its pipes, the chimneys and trees and telephone poles of the near neighborhood, to howling and shrieking."[23] Yet despite his focus on dreams, Edson's is not a purely surreal prose poetry, as Susan E. Hawkins and Donald E. Hardy have both noted. Hawkins observes that Edson's "fantasy world" is "slightly familiar in a way, never quite consistent, often gruesomely comic, never unorganized in the classically surreal way (one automatic, unconscious thought superseding another), and always challenging accustomed modes of thinking and perceiving."[24] What Edson reveals most fully is the manner in which behavior is scrupulously ordered by language. Indeed, as Hardy notes, "Instead of creating a surreal world through automatic writing as the European surrealists did, Edson in a sense presupposes a surreal world."[25] Yet for all his emphasis on the prose poem's similarity to dreams in their apparently unwilled creation, Edson's prose poems are artful constructions notable for their concentrated effects. Each of his works is remarkably condensed, its language moving in sometimes small increments to reveal absurd relations and absolutist patterns of language and behavior.

Beyond his concern with subverting literary genre through the dreamlike condensations of prose poems, Edson's discomfort with traditional form is demonstrated by his preoccupation with social structures as these master human subjects. Among the images of constricting forms that arise in his prose poems, perhaps none is more dominant than that of the house, which is associated with socially sanctioned representations of perception and experience. Edson has employed the image of the house throughout his career, to deepening effect, rooting out and investigating the many associations that the image bears. The simple image of the house as metonymy of the family is examined in repeated scenarios. He compares the house to cultural patterns that enable practices of oppressive violence, particularly within the contemporary family as a site of violence, neglect, and abandonment of children and the aged. In particular, the image of the house discloses calcified forms of human relationships as these are channeled by language. Susan Stewart's observations about nonsense procedures are especially cogent when applied to Edson's narratives:

If what is profound in metaphor has to do with its resonance to the un-conscious, it is nonsense that restores metaphor to consciousness by ex-posing it as a device, a formal procedure for making new meaning. . . .
[W]hat is made manifest through nonsense is form, procedure. When nonsense is engaged in reversing the metaphorical and the literal or the literal and the metaphorical, it is concerned with exploring the proce-dures by which the two domains are articulated.[26]

In Stewart's terms, we can see that Edson makes metaphor and formal practices "conscious." For all their superficial irrationality imposed through common nonsense devices, Edson's prose poems are put to the service of revealing procedures by which we may structure what we consider to be real and worthy of attention.

In Gaston Bachelard's meditations on the image of the house in *The Poetics of Space*, a book important to a number of poets of Edson's genera-tion,[27] the house affords "images of protected intimacy."[28] House imagery serves as "our first universe," "a real cosmos in every sense of the word."[29] Bachelard views houses as representative of beneficent stability. Yet Edson's houses, unlike those in Bachelard's discussion, are not sanctuaries; their structures are impositions that threaten psychic well-being. In opposition to Bachelard, houses in Edson's prose poems rupture mythologies of the pro-tective family. Repeatedly, those with any power in houses fail at sympathy and allow cultural structures to suffocate or absorb themselves or family members.

Like Stevie Smith, whose pictorial art often accompanies her poems, Edson sometimes provides commentary on his own preoccupations through his drawings and woodcuts. On the first page of *The Very Thing That Hap-pens*, he presents a drawing of the house-as-a-face, pinched at the eyes by a sloping roof, the forehead dwindling into a peak. The eyes, warily turned to the side, seem pressed in the vise of inescapable form. In like fashion, Edson's desperate personae are made painfully aware of their inability to escape limiting constructions. They are frustrated by the failure of inherited forms of thought and action to accommodate their desires. Their most sublime expectations dwindle into exhausted despair. As the speaker of "The Cere-mony" asks, "Had I suddenly become filled with God? Or was it a house falling in upon itself in the distance with a small sigh of dusty desperation?"[30]

He announces his preoccupation with physical, emotional, and mental boundaries in "Doctor House" in *A Stone is Nobody's*. In the prose poem the mysterious title character is equipped with windows in his forehead. The unnamed speaker contemplates his own position as he sits on the giant Dr. House's lapel, a pose that suggests his fixed perspective:

> Why does a house hold authority over what is *in* and what is *out*? Because I allow it, as I am the final authority over what is *in* and what is *out*—That I am able, while standing on Doctor House's green lapel, to say, I have not come into the world, but I have come out of a house.[31]

In Edson's prose poems the house serves as a barrier to fully lived experience, representing a site in which ritual structures of assumed authority dominate being. Bin Ramke makes the general point: "The prose poem is always a mediation as well as a meditation, and always concerns itself with authority."[32] Edson studies the means by which authority relies on freezing living being into readily controllable shape. Representations of mastery, in consequence, are shown to be absurdist. Those who seemingly demonstrate mastery over experience inevitably are trapped by their own structures—as if a perverse justice must be meted out regularly in his prose poems.

In a number of Edson's prose poems, the house as a representation of accepted structures of reality assumes uncanny proportions, sometimes proving impenetrable, at other times swallowing occupants. "I am not at home to you," declares a house in "The Unforgiven."[33] Family members in "The Terrible Angel" metamorphose into physical parts of their home, undergoing a horrible objectification; the baby turns into its cradle, the mother becomes part of the carpet (*IJ*, 5). Characters may restlessly move outside their houses; or, as in *The Intuitive Journey*, they may turn into parts of the structure itself, ingested as household objects; or they may be surrounded by the house-as-mausoleum. There would seem to be little room for even the illusion of human agency. In another prose poem that takes a Kafkaesque turn in its focus on an "arduous journey," an old man who wishes to leave his kitchen discovers that his route will lead him "through those remarkable conversations of the dining room; and through the living room, where murder is so common that to even notice it proves one the amateur" (*RWC*, 38). In "Conjugal" a man bends his wife into many shapes ("It is all so private"), at last pushing her into the bedroom wallpaper (*IJ*, 181). Inevitably, choices are limited within such houses, and lives are defined by a violence that is delivered or received without appropriate affective response, as if violence were an inevitable condition of contemporary life.

Often when their metaphorical houses collapse, characters discover themselves paralyzed and unable to imagine alternative structures or meanings. In "His House" a room proves a "dead end" filled with people who impose themselves upon Edson's hapless homeowner. The crowds foolishly seek salvation in a ready-made structure that condemns them to spiritual as well as physical claustrophobia:

> The householder closes the door on the room in full knowledge that nothing of value, in spite even of expectant crowds, ever happens in his house. . . . A dead end, a closed tunnel, which he enters and reenters like a foot stubbed endless times into a shoe: The house that walks the night through the dreamless dark. . . .
>
> (*RWC*, 36; ellipses Edson's)

Their expectations are futile. The householder's structure of meaning cannot satisfy their own unexamined desires.

Almost without exception, the house as primary figuration in these prose poems structures a movement toward objectification of persons. Edson's people are like the turtle who is "both the house and the person of that house" (*RWC*, 11). The house as a symbol of unchallenged forms of relationship not only confines bodily space but restricts the occupants' range of emotions and their ability to initiate any possible redemptive actions.

In the title poem of his seventh collection, "The Reason Why the Closet-Man is Never Sad," a house is composed only of closets, rooms where, ordinarily, not much actual living takes place: "Closets, you take things out of closets, you put things into closets, and nothing happens" (*RWC*, 62). If "nothing happens," the closet-man is not made to feel and thus can never be saddened. And if a closet-house makes for no feeling, perhaps (to reverse the figure) no feeling makes for strange houses, indeed, for closet-houses. Yet even in the event that we construct new houses, Edson intimates, we may underestimate the strength and persistence of our needs. In "The Cottage in the Woods," a man who builds his dwelling "near where the insect rubs its wings in song" discovers that his body towers over his house: "he must...lie unsheltered in the night even though a tiny bed, with its covers turned down, waits for him in the cottage" (*RWC*, 20). While social forms presumably exclude the needs of the character of "The Cottage in the Woods"—for he must lead his life without "a proper sense of scale"—the sexual sound of the insect buzzes wickedly in his ear.

Edson's preoccupation with the conventional structures of thought and feeling is connected unquestionably to his focus on language as it constructs representations of power. In particular, he delineates the formulae within language that ossify and reduce being, much as the houses of his prose poems constrain the lives of his afflicted characters. Susan E. Hawkins observes of Edson's prose poetry that "the logic of the syntax—the propositional nature of the subject-verb construct—is subverted again and again by unexpected and unexplained semantic choices."[34] His subversive choices, arbitrary as they may initially seem, are directed against habitual linguistic processes that distill the rules of social procedures. In "The Long Picnic," for instance, the assembled picnickers find that their idyll is a reverse Shangri-la, mysteriously aging each in turn. This process of aging occurs when "An official document blows through a forest between the trees over the heads of the picnickers." As time is telescoped, official words serve as a death sentence:

> A young man turns to his sweetheart. She's an old woman with white hair; her head bobs on her neck.
> The picnickers try to catch the document as it flies over their heads. But the wind carries it away.
> What is written on it is that *the summer is over* . . .
>
> (*RWC* 42; ellipses Edson's)

These amiable pleasure-seekers, the picnickers, cannot capture the all-pervasive force of textual form and are themselves subject to its veritable death sentence. They are, in Edson's buried pun, sentenced by a sentence. Because they cannot control words, words must control them.

When Edson casts women as houses—or as houselike housewives—he clarifies the cultural violence that is figured within language. In "The Rooming House Dinner," Edson creates a consumable landlady: "Someday it's stuffed shoes, stuffed with her own feet, served on a strange street where she is at last finding happiness way in the distance" (*RWC*, 63). In a later poem, "The House of Sara Loo," Edson builds an entire composition upon the woman-as-house metaphor.[35] Both genders are alternately solidified or expunged in his prose poems, but Edson's depiction of women resonates forcefully in terms of their "erasure." That is, despite the illusory solidity of the metaphorical form (woman as house; womb as home), women are often "eliminated" in scenarios. In portraying this process of metaphorical erasure turned actual erasure, Edson explores what Barbara Johnson calls "the coimplication of human violence and human figuration" in which "violence is structured like figure, and figure like violence."[36] Repeatedly, his characters' names suggest the ways in which they may be violently objectified. In "Mr. & Mrs. Duck Dinner," for instance, a woman who is compelled by domestic routine becomes the very object of her duty. A cook, she cooks her own and her husband's body in other people's houses (*IJ*, 36–37). Similarly, in another prose poem a daughter turns into a double bed to escape her parents' demands that she conform to their wishes (*RWC*, 22–23). While the body may rapidly metamorphose into an object as a means of partial escape from an intolerable authority figure, the powerless are only transformed in order to be acted upon all the more forcefully by the temporarily empowered. This process of objectification is similar, as Roland Barthes's observations suggest, to a process characteristic of much contemporary political ideology:

> Bourgeois ideology continuously transforms the products of history into essential types. Just as the cuttlefish squirts its ink in order to protect itself, [bourgeois ideology] cannot rest until it has obscured the ceaseless making of the world, fixated this world into an object which can be for ever possessed, catalogued its riches, embalmed it, and injected into reality some purifying essence which will stop its transformation, its flight towards other forms of existence.[37]

Edson dramatizes a violent arrest of such a "flight towards other forms of existence," in which the powerless become objects to be manipulated. Indeed, in his prose poems, he would counter or make visible a widespread ideology that posits stable and continuous identity (particularly the human constricted to the status of consumer) even while such an ideology would seek to create, in corporate culture, seemingly insatiable appetites for superficial novelty. An amnesia about personal and political history plagues his characters, many of whom are locked in absurd patterns of repetition, as if Edson were making clear the way a depthless sense of history, including personal history, makes inevitable both sterile behavior and a concretizing of identity.

Often violence in these prose poems is presented as unavoidable, for it is rooted in common language axioms that make humans into things for disposal. "Erasing Amyloo" is not only a primary instance of the erasure of the feminine, but extends upon and literalizes a simple language formula: an "unplanned" child is referred to in colloquial terms as a mistake; mistakes must be erased; the child must be erased. After Amyloo is actually erased by her father, the child's name is recalled incessantly by her mother.

When the mother points to Amyloo's possessions, her husband simply erases Amyloo's things as well. Next the father erases his wife's memory: "Bring your head over here and I'll erase Amyloo out of it." The mother is left with only a trace of Amyloo as detached name. Ironically, she then misidentifies her husband as Amyloo, his own being canceled within the marriage:

> The husband rubs his eraser on his wife's forehead, and as she begins to forget she says, hummm, I wonder whatever happened to Amyloo? . . .
> Never heard of her, says her husband.
> And you, she says, who are you? You're not my Amyloo, are you? I don't remember your being Amyloo. Are you my Amyloo, whom I don't remember anymore?. . .
> Of course not, Amyloo was a girl. Do I look like a girl?
> . . . I don't know, I don't know what anything looks like anymore. . . .
> (*RWC,* 26; ellipses Edson's)

Tellingly, the erased child is female. As we have seen, Edson presents victimized characters of both sexes, but his analysis of coercive power repeatedly makes clear the cultural vulnerability of women. Women are, in one way or another, expunged—by political will, by the patriarchal family, and by metaphorical construction.

Perhaps one reason why Edson's characters are so gruesomely disturbing and, often enough, very funny is that while they may destroy others or turn other humans into objects—or vice versa—they fail to attain their ultimate desires because, by and large, they have no memories. Or like Amyloo's mother, they may compulsively remember a name, a unit of language, but they cannot apply language correctly; they have no sense of a reality that might accept subtlety or fluency in naming or renaming and no memory of any psychic depth that allows them to make sense of their pasts. They only know that they must somehow pursue fragments of language. Yet they haven't the power fully to understand the ways in which they are used by language. The result is that they are compelled to reproduce the cruelties that have defined them.

Most often in these prose poems the family in particular is simply assumed to generate cruelty. Parents destroy children by demands for a ludicrous conformity; their attachment to a symbolic idea or expectation compels them to render their offspring into manipulable objects. Children are most often made into extensions of their parents and—or—effaced or assaulted. They may be the parents' expendable doubles or they may be locked in arcane and vicious rituals that emerge from familial ideology. Edson uses the generic names of Father and Mother as if they were symbolic of ritual-istic functions in families that are addicted to arbitrary displays of cultural authority. "Oh where is the Vomit Doctor?" a father asks in "Vomit." "At least when he vomits one knows one has it from high authority."[38]

In Edson's psychological exploration of the order of things, the old may be born to their children and identities in families may be wildly inter-changeable or murderously fixed. After a son tells his parents that he is a tree in "The Fall" they continue to believe his first assignment of self-iden-tity despite his later protests that he is not, after all, a tree. Characters find it frightening to alter their initial beliefs, despite evidence to the contrary and the vigorous protests of family members. In "The Broken Daughter" a child is made into a vehicle, the substitute for her mother as her father's secondary spouse of sorts, and yet simply another thing-in-the-house:

> This girl needs a whole new set of valves, and look at all those collision marks around her face, said the mechanic.

> I just want her fixed-up enough to use around the house; for longer trips I have my wife.[39]

In "The Birthday Party" parents who have given their daughter a pony for her birthday focus maniacally on the child's underpants. The parents con-cern themselves with excretion, as if a child is a synonym for waste. When the talking pony refuses to allow the little girl to ride him, the parents decide to make the pony their child and to present the pony with their daughter as a birthday present. They then dress the pony in their daughter's clothing and repeat their brutalities:

> They said to the pony, take this animal behind the house and mount it, for we have no wish to be advised as to what it is you wear on your excretory area.

> Soon the pony came around the house riding the naked little girl. She was crying.

> (*IJ*, 98)

How do Edson's characters cope in the threatening circumstances that he constructs for them? Rules that control characters are ironclad, and the unconscious logic of these rules seemingly cannot be subverted. At best, his characters must organize their identities from the most inadequate clues;

the self that emerges by bits and pieces from its environment is founded upon false logic. What is especially troubling and, paradoxically, sometimes darkly hilarious is the absence of all possible rescue for any of these characters. Most often they seek to control their situations by nullifying or disguising the difference between themselves and others that provokes fear. In "The Unscreamed Scream" a woman inhibits her impulse to express fully her anxieties about personal and ecological catastrophe by imagining ways to destroy her cat. "Set it on fire! Squeeze it in the door! . . . This is to keep herself from screaming" (RWC, 70). In "The Pregnant Ones" men usurp a woman's pregnancy and argue over the names of their children (RWC, 61). Hoping to quell their own anxieties about women and reproduction, they take on the pregnant woman's experience as their own and further suppress difference by presuming that their offspring will be male, that is, gender duplicates of themselves. Other characters are marionettes (one of Edson's preferred figures) yearning for a predictability that might lessen their apprehension. Even as the world ends, a speaker begs to be certain that he has correctly judged the contents of a walnut shell in "Please Don't Be a Walnut" (RWC, 58).

Other figures compulsively seek to be reassured by the ways in which their culture judges appearances. In "The Bride of Dream Man" Edson writes of the gruesomely comic marriage strategy of a loveless woman who believes that she accommodates her potential mate's assumed desires by engaging in an endless masquerade: "There was a fat woman who disguised herself as a fat woman." When the fat woman's mother asks about her daughter's strategy for the wedding night, the daughter replies with characteristic certainty, for she knows the "rules" of the conceptual/nuptial system that neutralize feminine identity. That is, she assumes that it is not her human identity but her sexual function that is most at issue:

> Then I'll take off the disguise, and he'll see that under the fat woman is another fat woman.
> And he'll think I'm an onion and not a woman.
> He'll think he's married an onion (which is another disguise), said the fat woman.
>
> Then what? sighed the mother.
>
> He'll say, oh what a kick, an onion with a cunt.

(IJ, 99)

Presenting herself as an infinitely layered and disguised form, the fat woman is never truly "present" for her illusorily perfect (and similarly unsubstantial) future mate, Dream Man. By disguising her true and threatening deviation from the cultural vision of an attractive woman's "appropriate" shape, she wittingly colludes with her objectification. She would rather be spoken of as an outrageous erotic novelty than as an actual fat woman.

Ironically, the curious power of "The Bride of Dream Man" stems, in part, from the resources of verse, its final, disquieting image accomplished in some measure through alliteration and assonance, its rapid speech exchanges reminding us of the line break's emphatic effects. Similarly, in "The Traveler" the extravagant symbolism of much modern and contemporary poetry is parodied, and sexual representation is literalized. A woman in the poem is a space to be opened, inside of which is a car that will drive a man to an airport, whereupon he will fly to an airstrip and enter a spaceship: yet more bewildering levels of representation dominate the experience of sexual difference. Concretizing sexual metaphor, Edson mocks the notion of the transparency of language: "Never mind if the spaceship is phallic, and that it thrusts into the dark vagina of space; he is, after all, only a traveler, not a symbolist" (*IJ*, 85). Of course, Edson is himself a self-conscious and witty symbolist of sorts—even while he would make us uncomfortable with his, or our, symbols and the manner in which they calcify meaning.

Edson's loathing of the ritualization of meaning takes its most unmistakable form in his images of excrement. For Edson, the family replicates waste; without autonomy family members have the ability only to destroy or to excrete. The fear the poems summon is that of the replication of experience or a perverse functionality. In an essay by Edson that seems to be part prose poem, part earnest exposition, he writes of the contemporary cultural view of human beings as little more than waste matter:

> The twentieth century, a country someplace in the universe; my species suffocating itself to death with its groin. Piling its redundancy beyond love or renewal; stool and child dropped with equal concern . . . We were our own excrement.[40]

He has telescoped his argument in the prose poem "One Man's Story," where it appears in the voice of "everyman":

> I tend to grow inside of my mother after my dad has with her. Nine months later I come out and start to mess on myself. Please forgive me, at

the time I don't know any better. But I do finally achieve the imago of my species. I enter my middle years; all the time growing toward my end. Finally I'm wornout and have become biological trash. Nature loses interest. I am alone . . .[41]

As these excerpts suggest, his characters may be abandoned as waste, which for Edson may be seen metaphorically as "form for its own sake" (*IJ*, 71). They are sensorily and intellectually stunted, commodified, and fixed in culture by the language conventions that they have not begun to question. To repeat and to miniaturize and, as a consequence, to become a form of waste: these are the threats to living being that Edson's work opposes. "In the vastness a man must miniaturize" (*IJ*, 135), he writes, his statement suggesting that a man is already seemingly miniaturized by the infinite. The compulsion to miniaturize further deadens any experience of being.

In terms somewhat like those in "Erasing Amyloo," Edson's prose poem "Counting Sheep" reveals an urge toward mastery and possession in which the living are arrested and diminished to suit the requirements of a predetermined form. In the prose poem a scientist has rendered sheep small enough to fit inside a test tube. The scientist then ponders the sheep as his commodities under glass:

> He wonders what he should do with them; they certainly have less meat and wool than ordinary sheep. Has he reduced their commercial value?
> He wonders if they could be used as a substitute for rice, a sort of woolly rice . . .
> He wonders if he just shouldn't rub them into a red paste between his fingers.
> He wonders if they're breeding, or if any of them have died.
> He puts them under a microscope and falls asleep counting them . . .
>
> (*IJ*, 12; ellipses Edson's)

The living animals are shown here as willfully reduced to suit the instruments of experimentation. Such shrinkage is an act of violence that provokes further violence, for certainly this prose poem is more than an elaborate extension of the worn phrase of its title. It dramatizes a state of mind that attempts mastery of living forms to a point where, paradoxically, the motivating mental state itself becomes self-destructive. In his own explication of the prose poem, Edson notes of the scientist's design on the sheep: "This is the kind of viciousness that comes of despair; and the kind of ecstasy of cruelty that has its target in the self."[42] Ironically, at the prose poem's conclusion the scientist is left asleep over his creations, his consciousness momentarily erased. In clear contrast to his scientist's manipulations in "Counting Sheep," Edson posits imaginative structures as in flux and ultimately unmastered: "I want to write the work that is always in search of itself, in a form that is always building itself from the inside out."[43] Of course one could argue that Edson conducts an experiment much like the scientist's: He shrinks or bloats shapes, hardening living forms into objects. But Edson's prose poem demonstrates the perversity of the very commodifications of being that he erects. For Edson, while language formulae inevitably constrict the unself-conscious user of language, imaginative freedom in language, at least provisionally, achieves the opposite. It allows us to project scenarios that clarify our situations and humble us properly.

Edson is one of the least attention-seeking of contemporary poets. As he wrote for *Contemporary Authors*: "Take it or leave it, I make it a point not to be a celebrity."[44] It is telling that one of the most comically abysmal of his characters is a variety of the writer, a realist who relies on aesthetic "rules" in the hope of self-glorification. The realist's act of assigning ongoing (if slowly evolving) identities is parodied by Edson—who inflates such techniques and creates immutable and self-destructive types. As Donald Hardy points out, Edson attacks "all kinds of self-aggrandizement."[45] In "Toward the Writing" he ruthlessly criticizes the self-important poet, lampooning the conventional view of the poet as inspired by a vision of death. In this prose poem the narrator advises would-be writers to acquire a mouse dead of disease as inspiration. Such advice, given another twist, may recall Edgar Allan Poe's statement that the most inspired subject for poetic contemplation is the death of a beautiful woman. In addition, Edson's prose poem may remind us of Wordsworth's conception of the poem as "emotion recollected in tranquility," for here Edson satirizes the re-presentation of emotion as inherently life-denying:

> Soon then, when grief has turned to art, you take the mouse to the writing table, and dip its rodent's tail into the ink . . .
> . . . But you will need many mice and many prayers. . . . And still the writing will wait, for the ritual is long . . .
>
> (*IJ*, 178; ellipses Edson's)

While the death of a homely female mouse is prescribed to make composition possible, it is the same rodent's body that becomes the writing instru-
ment—and a wonderfully absurd measure of writerly economy.

On occasion, Edson's writers are compelled toward mechanistic repetition, as if language, their formal master, demands its subjects' compulsive service. As Susan Stewart observes, repetition presents "the threat of
the self-generating, self-perpetuating machine. The machine's threat is the
disregard of context, an ongoingness despite the conditions of reality, the
'blindness' characteristic of the 'mental application' of any rule."[46] The
speaker of "The Ornament" is locked upon a wheel of such sterile recurrence:

> *How do I do it?* It just comes to me. Remarkable, isn't it? I mean the
> ornament of it. The fact is I live in the country and only pretend to be
> returning to my city apartment after a summer at my country home. It
> gives geographical significance, an animal with regular migrations. . . .
>
> . . . .
>
> All right, once more, and then I'm quits: I have just returned from my
> summer home in the country. . . . Somehow this still sounds so familiar . . .
>
> (*RWC*, 53)

This "realist" seeks ultimate control over language, as if creative expression
were simply composed of ornaments to be applied and manipulated at will.
Surely he does not follow Edson's advice about composition: "The idea is
to get away from obvious ornament, and the obligations implied therein."[47]
While the writer imagines an apartment for himself in New York City, such
an act of imagination proves only a tedious application of a stereotype about
a "typical" writer's lifestyle.

It is significant that Edson believes that the prose poem must be written
with speed if the author is to escape the inhibitions of self-censorship and
premeditation:

> This kind of creation needs to be done as rapidly as possible. Any hesita-
> tion causes it to lose its believability, its special reality; because the writing
> of a prose poem is more of an experience than a labor toward a product.[48]

Edson's focus on the deleterious effect of "any hesitation" in composition
hints at his own dread lest the linguistic structures that he erects eventually
enclose him. He takes seriously his own warnings about the solidification of
meaning. If the prose poem's form and content are to violate culturally

imposed structures of thought and feeling, so too must the author's process
of composition. For Edson, writing with speed allows him to rebel against
making "literature," a desire that, he believes, would result in the replication of formal and stylistic conventions. He trusts the process more than the
product, seeking "to find a prose free of the self-consciousness of poetry; a
prose more compact than the story-teller's; a prose removed from the formalities of *literature*."[49]

Given the way that Edson magnifies habitual forms of feeling and thinking without (at least overtly) positing a contrary, positive vision of human
relationship, might we think of him as espousing an antitranscendent poetic? Whereas Charles Wright investigates God, landscape, and language
with unappeased spiritual yearning, Edson more often dispels from his productions gestures of such overt transcendent desire. God is a puppetmaster
at best; and there is no origin, no setting, no display of social identity or
cultural mastery that grants ultimate meaning. When God enters Edson's
prose poems he appears as an omniscient taskmaster who defines and limits human fates and yet is indifferent to all phenomena except, perhaps,
entertainment. Edson disavows the centrality of human beings and the existence of a heaven as reward for good behavior. Visions above and beyond
the processes of human failure and diminishment, and, notably, of physical
indignity, prove inimical to his prose poetry. Yet the hurtling energy of his
prose poems, his reveling in an imaginative knowledge that assumes that
the very ground is quaking and everything is about to be lost—in such a
realm Edson claims his happiness, invoking what he calls, in a reference
that has undeniable spiritual foundations, "the Angel of Joy": "The sense
that all is passing away, even as I write this, that in a way the *new* means
death; this sense creates the Angel of Joy, which is for me the true Muse."
The imagination is not derived from a higher power for Edson but from an
interior power that moves close to, rather than well above, the opacity of
flesh and instinct.

In "The Tunnel," the title poem of his *Selected Poems*, Edson addresses
the issue of what seems to be his compulsive need to compose in the face of
despair:

> So I went tunneling into the earth, through darkness that penetra-
> tion only makes darker, faithful to the idea of light, said always to be at the
> end of tunnels; perhaps not yet lit, but in the universe moving in rendez-
> vous, thus to shimmer under the last shovelful of earth . . .[50]

> (ellipses Edson's)

For Edson, writing prose poems is "the joy when all other joys have failed." He argues in the same essay that "beyond the sense that all is lost is yet the real hope, the excitement of knowing that there is always a little more; and that *little more* is the joyous place from where one writes."[51] For Edson, the mind that makes and the mind that reads the prose poem encounter in clarified form a confining violence in culture that might otherwise appear natural and inevitable. The laughter or disgust that the prose poems evoke, responses elicited through our increased awareness of the grim halters of habit lowered over his limited characters' heads, may arouse our self-recognition.

Drawing rapidly upon his unconscious associations through the prose poem, Edson successfully provokes our laughter—although it is most often uneasy laughter, for his prose poems make available to consciousness the claustrophobia of both private and public relationships. In "A Man Who Makes Tears" he reflects on his own self-consciousness about preconceived form of any sort. Like Edson, the tear-maker constructs "tiny examples of the mystery that is large enough at times to swallow whole ships." Situated between conceptions of a self as both subject and object, the tear-maker is governed by linguistic and cultural imperatives. Caught in self-division, the tear-maker produces "tears which he thinks come out of his eyes from the memory of ponds and oceans. And he thinks they are tears of a marionette whose head is a jug of water with a sad face painted on it" (*RWC*, 45). Through his own "tiny examples," Edson would attempt, with full acknowledgment of the difficulty of his project, a larger liberation from linguistic convention. He prescribes what seems to be an impossibility: the abandonment of self in the act of writing. As he writes in another context, "We want to write free of debt or obligation to literary form or idea; free even from ourselves, free from our own expectations. . . . There is more truth in the act of writing than in what is written."[52]

3

"Dream Barker": Preoedipal Fusion and Radiant Boundaries in Jean Valentine

Most often, Jean Valentine's poems are not structured as quarrels nor do they have the ligature of narrative. Rather, they move through shifting images, often within the medium of dreams or in the first moments of her speaker's awakening. Dreams serve as the partial origin and model from which the poems take their aesthetic directions. "Our dreams are universal; our emotional and spiritual life is universal," Valentine maintained in an interview. "Because of that, it's just as much a communication, from one person to another, as if you were describing a landscape."[1] For Valentine, sleep catches "monsters" of the past and dissembles common certainties: "[T]he writing we remember does bring us something new, does in that sense trouble our sleeping selves, keeps us from settling down in whatever we thought last year, or last month."[2]

The progression of Valentine's books reflects her experimentation with constructing a new lyric that conveys some of the power that she ascribes to dreams. Selecting her first book, *Dream Barker*, for the Yale Series of Younger Poets Award, Dudley Fitts described Valentine as exhibiting "a quirkily singular intelligence, a fusion of wit and tenderness, subserved by an unusual accuracy of pitch and rightness of tone."[3] The lines of *Dream Barker* are thick with modifiers, internal rhyme, unusual diction, and an elaborate syntax. References to fairy tales and sexual life are prominent, and much of the volume's tone is that of anticipation. Her choice not only to evoke dream imagery but to use the medium of the dream as the point of reference would seem to be a surrealist inheritance that opens her poems to charged, nearly inexplicable situations. Appearing four years after *Dream Barker*, *Pilgrims* (1969) presents a stylistic departure with a stripped-down style, excised context, and more ambiguous syntax. The poems are less often clotted with

75

modifiers than those of *Dream Barker* but more stark in their pronounce-
ments. She records a curious receptivity on the part of her speakers, particularly in the midst of domestic catastrophe. In *Pilgrims* her speakers send
out bulletins that describe their embattled positions, and the poems' styles
reflect a conceptual shift, moving from the metaphors of social and sexual discovery characteristic of Valentine's first book to a dispiriting vision
of marriage that is reflected in spare, frequently brief, nearly enervated
poems.

After *Dream Barker*, Valentine's poems suggest tenuous psychological states
through unexplained contextual references and expanded use of white spaces
and staggered lines. Increasingly, she has thinned connective passages and
omitted logical connections in her poetry as if she were seeking a new lyric
that might reflect the vagaries of selfhood in psychological transition. The
poems evince what she calls "a pull against the poem as a sort of finished,
well-wrought statement."[4] As one of her best critics, Philip Booth, points
out, her poetry "is composed of the most complex permutations and com-
binations of silence and sound, of variantly paced line-ends and caesurae,
and of a brilliantly individual syntax."[5] Although some of her poems are
given dates of composition, the events described in them seem to occur out
of time or appear as if they are cryptic reworkings of her essential themes
cast in a highly subtle, idiosyncratic poetic. As Steven Cramer puts it,
"[U]nlike typically surrealist poems with their stock footage of De Chirico-
esque landscapes, Valentine's compact lyrics inhabit the *thought* of the unconscious—its paralogistic reasoning and dislocating jump-cuts."[6] Often
her poems are infused by a personal voice that refuses the rather dour oracular overtones common to deep imagists. Nor are the voices that she assumes the sort that reflect autobiographical convention, as she pointed out
in an interview: "One thing I feel sure of about the use of the self is that
while there are poems [of her own] that may use the 'I' with very little sense
of the 'real self' in them, there are *no* poems that present the 'real self'
precisely, 'as is,' as one would try to in, say, an autobiography."[7] Gaps in
sense-making that we may readily detect in her poems suggest the disjointed
quality of interior reverie and reflect her engagement with presenting feeling states that are recalcitrant to language.

Helen Vendler's remarks on the significance of stylistic change in poets
cast light on Valentine's own experiments in style:

> It is still not understood that in lyric writing, style in its largest sense is best
> understood as a material body. When a poet puts off an old style (to speak

for a moment as if this were a deliberate undertaking), he or she perpe-
trates an act of violence, so to speak, on the self. It is not too much to say
that the old body must be dematerialized if the poet is to assume a new
one.

In the body of Valentine's writing we see a "thinning out" of textual materiality. After *Dream Barker* her poems increasingly appear to float in white
space, as if about to be lifted from the page. If we attend to Vendler's analogy between the body of the poem and the poet's bodily self, we see Valentine
as lightening and diffusing her sense of corporeality, rendering an ethereal
poetry that revolts against the materiality of the body and the text and their
combined gravity.

As we shall see, stylistic change in Valentine's poetry is linked with one
of her primary themes: abandonment. In Vendler's conception, stylistic
revision is motivated by the implications of abandonment: "The fears and
regrets attending the act of permanent stylistic change can be understood
by analogy with divorce, expatriation, and other such painful spiritual or
imaginative departures."[8] In other words, Valentine's commitment to stylistic change, to a progressive purification of her body of work, is inscribed
on her poems through her overt subject of abandonment. Stylistic change—
as a form of abandonment—is reinforced by Valentine's thematic exploration of domestic and cultural desertions.

Valentine is a poet of departures, especially of the desertion of women
by men, of separation and divorce, and of the death of friends and family
members. She began her career speaking from the position of a woman
who experiences a sudden and painful abandonment. The cause of this
desertion is not acknowledged; it is the fact of abandonment itself that marks
her early poems. The speaker's losses, however, would seem connected to a
primary loss, a traumatic initial wound, and the task of the poems, particularly the later poems, has been to avoid occluding or denying such a psychic
wound even while moving outward to consider the manifold losses of others and thus defeating solipsism.

I have situated Valentine at the midway point in this book for a number
of reasons. In some of her most important poems she presents the essential
drama of desertion by a beloved and as such she offers a clarifying perspective of abandonment in relationships. I also introduce her work at this juncture
because she is the most focused of these poets, as I shall discuss, on curatives,
that is, on partial remedies for the trauma of desertion that threatens to

overwhelm her personae and that allows the menace of self-destruction to erupt on the periphery of her poems. As such, she offers a vivid example of a poet who directly takes impetus from imagining and responding to a state of being severed from crucial affective ties. Questions of origin are complicated by the affective ties to the maternal in this poetry (to be discussed later)—ties that complicate assertions of individualist identity and that foreclose on any possibility of ultimate mastery over self and others. As I shall suggest, Valentine's rather complexly evolved vision of human relationship would dismantle claims of power deployed in force over others.

Valentine's first collection is immersed in a young woman's thwarted love quest. The poems of *Dream Barker* deal in part with initiation into sexuality, which is presented as a language to be learned, as in the poem "Sex": "And the thing itself not the thing itself, / But a metaphor."[9] The opening poem, "First Love," mourns lost intimacy founded on bodily pleasure "before the world began." Here the sea bottom is a turning world without boundaries, a sort of preoedipal seabed. The persona insists that she alone witnesses the withdrawal of a seductive other, a near second self whose animalistic features are varied to the point that we cannot entirely identify the creature:

> Gone your feathery nuzzle, or was it mine,
> Gone your serpentine
> Smile wherein I saw my maidenhood smile,
> Gone, gone all your brackish shine,
> Your hidden curl, your abandoned kill,
> Aping the man, liebchen! my angel, my own!
>
> (*DB*, 3)

This "glue-eyed prince" is internalized as heart, love object, and as "dearest black nudge." The self and the other seem to be reflective doubles, monstrous in the way that mermaids are monstrous: otherworldly, both beast and human. Implicitly, the poem's drama involves what used to be called sexual deflowering, with the violated virgin now an "abandoned kill." But the poem's insistent metaphors convey a womblike state of initial security, conflating mother and lover, and the deflowering male with a trickster angel, a representative of sorts of the symbolic order who, as we shall see in Julia Kristeva's formulations, disrupts the mother-child relationship.

The title poem of *Dream Barker* reveals in more overt form the qualities that first brought Valentine attention in 1965. In the poem a woman ar-

rives with a man in a watery underworld in which they will make a marvel-
ous purchase:

> *What'll you have?* you said. Eels hung down,
> Bamboozled claws hung up from the crackling weeds.
> The light was all behind us. To one side
> In a dish of ice was a shell shaped like a sand-dollar
> But worked with Byzantine blue and gold. *What's that?*
>
> *Well, I've never seen it before,* you said,
> *And I don't know how it tastes.*
> *Oh well,* said I, *if it's bad,*
> *I'm not too hungry, are you? We'd have the shell . . .*
> *I know just how you feel,* you said
>
> And asked for it; we held out our hands.
> *Six Dollars!* barked the barker, *For this Beauty!*
> We fell down laughing in your flat-bottomed boat,
>
> And then I woke up: in a white dress:
> Dry as a bone on dry land, Jim,
> Bone dry, old, in a dry land, Jim, my Jim.
>
> (*DB,* 48)

In the phantasms of the unconscious the couple discovers and agrees to buy
the shell out of a love of beauty rather than hunger. The dream barker puts
into language their desires: *"Six dollars!"* barked the barker, *"For this Beauty!"*
In his cry the barker links the shell to materiality and flesh. At the center of
the dream, the shell is "shaped like a sanddollar / But worked with Byzantine blue and gold"; it is formed as if it were of determinate value. It is, at
the same time, "worked with," an object reminiscent of crafted art, specifically of Byzantine splendor. Yet after the happy laughter of the lovers as
they consider the shell in "Dream Barker," the woman is abruptly abandoned. Given that the man and the woman's emotions and perceptions
had been unified, the disruption of such intimacy is mystifying. The concluding stanza's partial stops and repetition of *dry* (four times within two
lines) underscore the suddenness with which the dream ends. An abrupt
shift into the daytime world occurs, a daytime that is as extreme as the
dream world in its opposite evocation of dryness and sterility.

In this and other poems, including "Miles from Home," "Déjà-vu," and "Asleep Over Lines from Willa Cather," Valentine recreates a psychic journey that most often ends in failure and dissolution. Union between individuals is followed by expulsion or abrupt departure—a movement from fusion to disunity and a recognition of what seems like lethal difference, as if cycles of connection followed by disunity must be reenacted perpetually.

At the same time that Valentine writes in what she considers to be the "landscape" of dreams, we cannot ignore the gendered dynamics of the dramas she presents. The moments of desire that end in disappointment are most often stories of womanly love. Her speakers' greatest psychic apprehensions occur in dreams in which the same situation repeats itself: a heightened feeling of unity is experienced with another, followed by stunning abandonment. To the protagonist, abandonment seems incomprehensible, somewhat like a mysterious and implacable force of nature.

How are we to make sense of Valentine's poems in which such abandonments figure prominently? The puzzle at the heart of many of Valentine's poems is uncomfortably close, I shall argue, to a daughter's assimilation to the symbolic order and concomitant mother-loss, as the process is described in Julia Kristeva's writings. It is not the actual death of the mother in the early poems that is registered, but a daughter's inevitable psychological separation from her mother, amounting to a first wound that is felt again with each subsequent loss. Valentine's personae are abandoned in ways that appear inexplicable, just as the daughter's first movements away from her mother as she enters the symbolic order may appear unavoidable and mystifying. Subsequent loves are seen in Valentine's poems through the scrim of maternal love.

Dream Barker is a highly accomplished first book, and Valentine's preoccupations are clearly marked in it: a fixation on bodily process and a keen connection to what seems to be preoedipal memory evinced by womb imagery and fusion dramas. After her first book, her poems increasingly appear telegraphic, like faint trail marks, each with its connections and contexts partly sutured, just as the self that the poems present seems cut from a beneficent source that in its doubleness and insistent womblike imagery appears allied to the maternal. Valentine's imprinting of the maternal performs as a first level in the poems. In her poetry, "first love" is maternal love; later loves bring to the surface the most archaic of desires for fusion, which may be founded in the mother-child relationship.

In *Black Sun* Julia Kristeva discusses the difficulty of separation from the maternal, illuminating similar elements in Valentine's poetry:

The Freudian notion of *psychic object* . . . is a memory event, it belongs to
lost time, in the manner of Proust. It is a subjective construct, and as such
it falls within the realm of a memory, elusive to be sure and renewed in
each current verbalization, that nevertheless is from the start located not
within a physic space but within the imaginary and symbolic space of the
psychic system. . . .

    Such a linguistic and temporary phenomenology discloses . . . an
unfulfilled mourning for the maternal object.[10]

Valentine builds a poetics that explores relationships between men and
women through the lens of maternal loss—as if maternal loss were a vague
memory, or partly sensed, partly intuited. As Kristeva suggests in more
general terms, such a "memory" is "elusive to be sure and renewed in each
current verbalization." Valentine's poems are predicated in part not only
upon englobed womb-water images that suggest preoedipal experience, as
in "First Love," but in traces of an inchoate memory of the presymbolic
that is reflected in some of the very difficulties of Valentine's style, with its
elided references and opaque or missing context. As Kristeva notes:

> [I]n any poetic language, not only do the rhythmic constraints, for ex-
> ample, perform an organizing function that could go so far as to violate
> certain grammatical rules of a national language and often neglect the
> importance of an ideatory message, but in recent texts, these semiotic
> constraints . . . are accompanied by nonrecoverable syntactic elisions; it is
> impossible to reconstitute the particular elided syntactic category (object
> or verb), which makes the meaning of the utterance undecidable. . . .[11]

In her examination of "the mother-child relationship" Kristeva asks that
we "consider what this presymbolic and trans-symbolic relationship to the
mother introduces as aimless wandering within the identity of the speaker
and the economy of its very discourse. Moreover, this relationship of the
speaker to the mother is probably one of the most important factors producing interplay within the structure of meaning as well as a questioning
process of subject and history."[12] For Valentine, the memory of the
presymbolic, the preoedipal that infuses experience between lovers, is inscribed in the linguistic "cells" of her poems and played out in images and
narratives. As such, the question of abandonment is larger than an issue of
heterosexual relations; it would seem backlit in Valentine's poems by a felt
quality of absolute abandonment, a sensation of desertion by the maternal
that is devastating. The poems would act like thin membranes stretching

over the bottomlessness of primary human need. Yet finally this abandonment is transpersonal; among individuals she would suggest similar needs founded on the common loss of preoedipal unity.

Valentine's work, however, does not capitulate entirely to a longing for a state prior to the acquisition of language, no matter how much we may intuit the lack that she is drawn to insinuate. Her poems' contrary impulses involve vigorously imagining relationship beyond the vaguely felt perimeters of a primary identification. The conceptual burden that she assigns herself in poems lies in imagining psychological boundaries between individuals that reveal difference. Boundaries in her poems by her midcareer tend to be framed as light, as radiantly permeable visual phenomena, marking out but not isolating one realm of experience or being from another.

In *Pilgrims* there is little hope of vital relationships between individuals. After the poems of disrupted fusion in *Dream Barker*, Valentine's second book records disillusion and isolation; any resonant feeling is menaced. The self here seems as if it has been "skinned"—alternately left raw and vulnerable, or inured to feeling. In contrast to *Dream Barker*, *Pilgrims*, as its title suggests, is a more penitential book in which the primary persona has seemingly lost her way. The sensuality of Valentine's first book appears to have been deliberately expunged, as if the poet were to remake a poetic selfhood in her second book, beginning only with the most bare rudiments. Her first book had absorbed confessionalist influence in its somewhat bold dealing with sexual feelings and bodily images. *Pilgrims* subsequently divests the lyric of much of the sensory richness that her early readers had come to expect as Valentine rebuilds self and her relationship to language.

Pilgrims opens with exhaustion and boredom in intimate relations, recasting Valentine's theme of abandonment:

> even you, Prince, gray
> around the mouth and tired of calling,
> tired of briars, tired of them,
> had ridden away.

Her couples reflect not smugly but rather sadly on their similarities. Now even good manners amount to censorship: "Out of decency no one spoke."[13] There is little insistence on the prominence of bodily pleasure for her "dumb, / dressed, affectionate" couples (*P,* 17). Such characters are distanced from their own desires. They cannot comprehend the source of their losses:

"Archaically cut off. Antarctic miles" (*P,* 44). Crisis informs the poems, but each contingency is met with simple gestures of tenderness or bafflement. In "Fireside" Valentine plays upon foxfire as the "organic luminescence from decaying wood," the "light" of marriage. Yet marriage and domesticity offer a tranquility underwritten by ambivalence and stultification. The fox referred to in the poem—living, quick, symbolic of cunning and sexuality—is pointedly not *of* the house, and while a husband and wife are "nicer than God" (*P,* 4), their inertia and passivity hardly seem attractive.

In *Pilgrims* the myth of Orpheus and Eurydice proves a defining one in its evocation of abandonment. The stalled underworld body of Eurydice (which Valentine spells *Euridice*), and the torn body of Orpheus after he has been dismembered by the maenads are conflated in "Orpheus and Euridice." The poem echoes the earlier "Dream Barker," suggesting that abandonment is a template of this work. In the poem, Valentine has her Eurydice speak, conferring presence upon the mythological figure who is confined to darkness and silence in Ovid and Virgil. For all outward appearances, Orpheus in mythological renderings and in the poem's revision of the myth has not meant to abandon Eurydice; his journey to the underworld has been accomplished at great cost to him. And yet by disobeying the injunction of the god of death he has made inevitable Eurydice's final death, now "unchangeable." At the poem's conclusion, as Valentine's Eurydice speaks, the lovers are reunited:

> *What we had, we have.* They circle down.
> You draw them down like flies.
> You laugh, we run
> over a red field, turning at the end to blue air,—
> you turning, turning again! the river
> tossing a shoe up, a handful of hair.
>
> (*P,* 15)

We might note that, in Valentine's retelling of the myth, the lovers ultimately join one another only after they have despaired utterly. The uniting of Orpheus and Eurydice is not told as a story of simple salvific hope, but of reunion achieved after absolute loss, a disembodied union in which the lovers witness their own fragmentation, their own ruin, or, with Orpheus, his willed self-destruction. As Eurydice insists, this is "our underworld." She recounts in almost primerlike simplicity their mutual meeting in death accomplished by the dismemberment of Orpheus's body in the river Hebrus.

In speaking of the dismemberment of Orpheus's body, she is given a subject position in a narrative that depends on gaps, fragments, and points of omission, as if the poem's style echoes one of its last events: Orpheus's dismemberment.

In *The Messenger* another retelling of the myth occurs among Valentine's translations of poems by the Dutch poet Huub Oosterhuis. In her translation Orpheus eventually is without any sense of bearings or boundaries as he continues to walk ahead of Eurydice:

> He walks and no longer knows
> whether or not he did look back
> and where the earth is
> underneath   above.[14]

And in yet another reworking of the myth's essentials in "Turn (2): After Years," Valentine re-presents the gestures she establishes as intimate in "Orpheus and Euridice." Recognition of the other, now in Martin Buber's terms, means that some new understanding between women and men may be made possible. She records the process of differentiation, allowing identities to break from fusion and dependency:

> Now I can turn,
> —now, without want, or harm—
> turn back to the room, say your name:
> say: *other*   say, *thou*. . . .

> (*M*, 49)

Valentine rewrites the act of turning—the defining and the destructive act in the myth—now as neither dismissal of another nor as fusion with another, but as recognition of separate identity. Here, the act of turning that had sentenced Eurydice to her second death signals a transition, not only into the fertile unconscious but toward an eventual recognition of the other's difference.

It is telling that this poetry continually thwarts attempts by personae to possess the objects of their desires or to be possessed by them. Just as Charles Wright searches for signs of the unpossessable transcendent, Valentine's lovers, grateful for the smallest warmth, must discover a means beyond possession of the other. Often, however, her speakers are neglected or rejected by those with whom they had been intimate. Their desertion is especially painful because their sense of being is inscribed by a vision of psychological and physical oneness that is only possible with the maternal; they are at least vaguely aware of feeling states of ultimate union that are irrevocably lost to them.

Ordinary Things (1974) continues stylistically in the vein that Pilgrims established, but here Valentine overtly works with the motif of separation and loss of meaning after the breakup of a marriage. She would illuminate common motives and daily acts; her catalogs of objects and actions are characterized by a light-infused, otherworldly Rilkean sensibility. This emptying out of meaning causes anxiety that must be met with quiet words and a tentative groping beyond the isolation that was established in Pilgrims. The tone of desperation that we hear in Valentine's poems is modified by her attempt to find spiritual meaning in the ordinary, as her title, taken from Oosterhuis's "Twenty Days' Journey," underscores.

In Ordinary Things Valentine investigates the elementary notions of physical boundaries as these suggest cultural boundaries. When poems reflect politics—notably in reference to the Vietnam War—events are experienced as personal and textual, through the speaker's reading of newspapers or viewing of television. The poems are saturated with a nearly depressive silence, and just as the Vietnam War is viewed from a distance, that is, from newspaper and televised reports, the book suggests distance in personal intimacy, observing personal collapse in the midst of cultural collapse.

At the periphery of many of the poems lurks an impulse toward self-destruction, and with The Messenger (1979) it becomes clear that Valentine writes of self-destruction more often than many poets in her generation. A number of Valentine's poems throughout her body of work refer to suicide, among them: "For a Woman Dead at Thirty," "He Said," "Susan's Photograph," "What Happened," "Still Life: In the Epidemic," "Ironwood," and "To Plath, To Sexton." Her speakers do not consider any sort of abjection from the psyche of the threatening self-destructive complex or the menacing other. Rather, they prescribe faith in the psyche's ability, over time, to absorb and transform threats to survival, particularly those threats that emerge from internal compulsion. The notational character of many of the poems intimates that Valentine is intent on calming a troubled spirit; the poems are prayerlike minims for survival. Like Wright, Valentine is drawn to intimations of divinity. Yet her divinity, unlike Wright's, is not transcendent. Instead, divinity is sought through physical responses, a longing for what seems to be a lost realm of pacific, mammalian unity, a refuge against the danger of self-destruction that appears on the edges of her poems.

In this context, it is instructive to compare Valentine's early poetry to Sylvia Plath's last poems. Plath, of course, is a poet of a very different order, but wittingly or not, Valentine in her early career was shadowed by strategies that are familiar from Plath's work. Although Valentine did not read Plath's work until after Plath's 1963 suicide,[15] the image of "SS men's heels" in "New York April 27, 1962" from *Dream Barker* recalls us to Plath's use of Nazi imagery in her final poems. The bracing, nursery-rhyme-like rhythms and the juxtaposition between the image of tender babies and the solemnity of an archetypal bell ringing "in thin air" (*DB*, 26) are also reminiscent of Plath. Another poem, Valentine's "Déjà-vu," contains direct accusatory lines echoing Plath's "Daddy": "And now You! / Now You let me know it was always You" and "I'd laugh but I never, never loved You" (*DB*, 10). More fully, Valentine's "For a Woman Dead at Thirty" forces an inevitable comparison to Plath's suicide, for in the poem a young Plath-like suicide is presented in a "side mirror"; this suicide's vision is a product not only of romantic individualism but of "bungled fever"—of something akin to genius, but a genius that mistakes psychic suffering for poetic resonance. The poem essentializes its Plath-like subject as a "blazing / Negative" and a "wavering light in water, / Water I stir up with a stick: wavering rot." For Valentine, Plath would seem to be a sister of sorts: a fellow contemporary and countrywoman, and yet Plath is not only blazing but wavering, and suicide is symbolized as a descent into decay and an efflorescence of confessionalist self-destruction.

Valentine's most direct description of the confessionalist legacy takes place in the penultimate stanza of the poem, running through to the concluding lines:

> O my sister!
>   even if I'd known,
> All I could have said was that I know.

(DB, 4)

The suicide of this young woman is met with comprehension, the poem makes clear. Yet the final lines suggest helplessness in the face of despair's clarity; they announce a form of solidarity with the woman who commits suicide but they do not suggest a remedy. The poem thus offers both recognition and a declaration of difference. Plath's images of destruction and exorcism are avoided by Valentine's lights—by virtue not only of temperament, perhaps, but by virtue of another sort of reasoning. That is, Valentine does not consider psychic material destroyable, and the hope of nullifying such material strikes her as naive. For Valentine, the identification of psychic trauma is possible, however, which amounts to an act of receptivity that may make positive psychological transformation possible.

Plath's visceral sense of threat, of the feminine under siege, and Plath's display of sexuality: from these Valentine has surely learned. Certainly, she absorbed Plath's externalization of psychic dynamics. Yet while Valentine works with images of extremity, she handles them with a sense of the combustible nature of her materials. As we have noted, Valentine has written a number of poems that overtly deal with suicide, but she writes "away" from the self-destructive impulse. A survival instinct, however tenuous at times, can be perceived in most of her poems. Plath, however, must have seemed to be uttering a negative mantra while Valentine sought a psychological security that did not violate her integrity as a poet.

After her first book, Valentine expunged even brief reminders of the violence that we may associate with Plath from her own poetic and increasingly presented an effaced speaker. The "I" in her poems is muted, intent on entering into the same ordinary space of comprehension as the reader. Such gestures convey a disbelief in the absolute centrality of the first-person pronoun. Already in "Sunset at Wellfleet," from her first book, nature assumes its own self-referentiality, whereas the self notes an essential "emptiness" that differs markedly from confessionalist display:

> The rattling bay runs night and day *I, I, I,*
> Over and over, turning on itself: there,
> Where it curls on emptiness: there I sing.
>
> (*DB,* 11)

Valentine's references to the confessional poets in an interview makes clear that not only their poetry but their lives deeply influenced her. "I used to be scared by the writers who went ahead of me—so many of them were alcoholic or mentally ill or suicidal." Initially, the role of the artist seemed linked for her to self-destruction. "I had a deep feeling, a deep fear about being an artist, that it would lead me right off the edge of a cliff into death, not just into alcoholism or mental illness, but that I wouldn't survive."[16] Despite such inhibitions, she allowed herself to be affected by confessionalist methods but not confessionalist solutions. Valentine's "Anaesthesia," for instance, focuses on a woman who is visited after childbirth by contemporary versions of evil fairies—a plot that would surely interest both Sexton

and Plath. But Valentine modifies the fairy story in which the birth of a
child draws down a jealous fairy. Here her irreal creatures are marked by
artifice. They are masked and self-destructive, plantlike in their bowers,
rooted in what seems to be the deepest layers of the speaker's psyche. Immediately the poem's title, "Anaesthesia," accomplishes at least two tasks. It
suggests the dreamlike and numbing effects of anaesthesia on the speaker
after she gives birth, her vision prompted by the surreal strangeness of her
drugged state. In addition, the title refers to the drama of many of these
poems: the temptation to deaden and destroy is shown to be ineffective, a
form of anesthesia that cannot successfully accompany a "surgery" to re-
move the intimidating other. The quietness of Valentine's concluding lines
with their proselike rhythms may seem more horrific than her nearly gothic
earlier drama of women imaged as suicides/trees in these lines:

> . . . not-women they were suicides, trees, soft,
> pale, freckled branches bending over her—
> I knew them as my own, their cries
> took on the family whiskey voice, refusal,
> need,—their human need peeled down, tore,
> scratched for her life—

Her response to these figures had been like that of a prince in "Sleeping
Beauty" (a fairy tale particularly resonant in this context) who must make
his way through a barrier of thorns:

> I hacked and hacked them apart—
>
> then who knows
> when you murder things like that
> who comes in and takes over[17]

In murdering rather than in understanding these figures, Valentine notes
that their evil influence has not been conquered. Unfortunately, her speaker
may have only allowed some other power to "take over." The poem's resolution, a refusal of malevolent glee or open challenge, points up the inadequacy of confessionalist gestures that would make a show of extracting
negative psychic complexes. Valentine's is a profoundly recursive poetry;
feelings of guilt and shame return, and the slaying of past demons fails.
Early trauma is not excised (although perhaps it may be metamorphosed)

and the seeming elimination of inner demonic forces opens the way to conceivably worse forces.

The Messenger clearly announces its link to *Ordinary Things*. "Susan's Photograph" and "Outside the Frame" are reprinted in *The Messenger* from the previous volume, emphasizing at the book's opening the survival of at least one aspect of Valentine's persona and the defeat of self-annihilating impulses. What accompanies the more expansive vision that follows is a notable stylistic change: Valentine's willingness to entertain in the lyric a larger repertoire of techniques. *The Messenger* is a breakthrough book, signaling a broadening of theme and a greater inclusiveness of voices—a recovery from the vague inertia and overly purified sensibility evident in her previous two books. She experiments more fully with prose passages, infusions of quotations, and a patterning of white space within lines and between unevenly sized stanzas. This is a more plentiful vision than can be seen in either *Pilgrims* or *Ordinary Things*, and the book centers less often on despair than Valentine's earlier books; instead, it attempts to find sustaining potentials: the solace of meaningful solitude counterpoised by meaningful friendship. In this collection more than any other, she considers the discipline of friendship as it demands imagination and understanding rather than psychological fusion. Friendship reduces shame and creates an answering other. Friends are portrayed as offering opportunities to engage with otherness, evading the lure of projection and fusion that is more immediately tempting in romance.

"Writing was like having an imaginary friend,"[18] Valentine has commented in an interview. In "Sanctuary" she addresses her crossed desire for both meditation conducted alone and for warm friendship in which the other is not mastered or possessed: "*To wait. To imagine.*" Otherwise she suggests: "not seeing each other; seeing instead some mask / or sign; consenting to be some mask or sign" (*M*, 45). *The Messenger* offers a strategy that had only been implied in earlier poems. She explores more fully the gradual development of meaning and the possibility of a beneficent vision of the self's future, in which the messenger of the title is not only symbolic of the future as it discloses itself, but a welcoming spirit of the present.

The Messenger makes more clear Valentine's attraction to the poetry of Elizabeth Bishop, whose sense of emotional homelessness is similar to Valentine's. In an interview Valentine called Bishop's poetry "both simple and endlessly resonant with meaning."[19] We have already noted Valentine's early absorption of Plath's influence, and it is possible to see in Valentine's poetry unmistakable signs of an Emily Dickinson-like concern for spiritual sustenance, telegraphic syntax, omission of context— and even terror. (In Bishop such characteristics are muted; we must, in a sense, bend to hear them in the quiet economy of her lines.) What Bishop offers Valentine, in contradistinction to Dickinson or Plath, is the example of a recent predecessor who explores ways of comforting and forgiving the beleaguered psyche. Bishop reveals the poem as labor toward survival rather than self-destruction; the poem serves for imaging an ordered sanity that nevertheless acknowledges threats to sanity. That is, the Bishop that Valentine appropriates for her own purposes is a benign elder of sorts and, more fully, an imaginative force for self-integration.

When Marianne Moore characterized Bishop as "spectacular at being unspectacular" she might have been describing a certain element in Valentine's poetry, especially her ability to create unassuming authorial presences. Yet while Bishop is an intensely visual poet, Valentine prefers to suggest the invisible. She explores the arbitrary and tentative ways that meanings may accrue, the way "the water-lit, dotted lines of home start coloring in" (*M*, 6). She renders contingency and disintegrating presence more often than does Bishop. The details of landscape, the grains of her descriptions: there is seldom the illusion of anything leisurely about accumulations of details in Valentine. From their inception, moments are bound toward heightened psychological significance. As Valentine remarked in an interview: "I don't think that poets are that interested in recording things. I think they're interested in going through them, going through them like doors. Maybe it is to a world we're seeking, not a world we already know."[20] Her statement underscores her propensity for imagining beyond immediacy into the "interior" of an event.

In "Snow Landscape, in a Glass Globe" (a homage to Bishop) Valentine mimics Bishop's "questions of geography" and of instability and direction. Her persona meditates on the figure of a Chinese woman in the glass globe, "calm at her work, / carrying her heavy yoke / uphill, towards the distant house."[21] Valentine describes a serene but difficult exertion with shelter set at a distance, alluding to Bishop's and her own poetic. Both share a difficult, continual labor—a commitment to crafting the quietly revelatory poem—that is beset by longings for security, particularly for a psychic home of sorts. In the poem's miniaturization of an englobed distance, the earth remains "living" and the process of writing unites and enlivens. In another poem alluding to Robert Lowell as well as to Bishop, "Barrie's

Dream, the Wild Geese,"[22] Valentine mourns the loss of Bishop, Lowell, and their generation of American poets. Finally, it is an appreciation of intense poetic labor that she values as their legacy.

Valentine's sixth book, *The River at Wolf* (1992), opens to greater grief than any of her earlier collections. With the progression of her books— from the early bridal and motherhood poems of *Dream Barker*, to contemplations of difficult marital separations in *Pilgrims* and *Ordinary Things*, to her new concentration on friendship and salvific meditations in *The Messenger* and, in most recent years, an explicit summoning of the elegiac—she has returned as well to her first issues. In *The River at Wolf* she allows for the images of intense physicality and unexplained departure that marked her first book. Yet the poems seem less evanescent than much of her previous work and exhibit some of the earthy quality of her debut collection without sacrificing the spiritual intimations of later volumes. Poems in *The River at Wolf* are generally shorter than much of her work in *The Messenger*—as if Valentine had gained immediate, telegraphic access to unconscious thought. In particular, *The River at Wolf* may prove to be her strongest collection because the maternal, so often sotto voce in other collections, is projected more fully in elegies that take their momentum from the death of Valentine's mother. The maternal is embodied in an actual woman but one whose being extends into larger dimensions as a friend, philosopher, teacher, and a source allied to the divine. Valentine has brought to bear all her aesthetic lessons from previous volumes by recognizing an initial wound that is formed by a source of sustenance's abandonment. In contemplating AIDS in several poems she indirectly reflects on her own experiences with isolation and depression—and with a failure to name and identify and thus to objectify experience in a way that might allow for a release from suffering.

Frequently she writes of threshold states of being or of psychological and spiritual containment, states reflecting her shifting relation to the maternal. Valentine's mother is externalized in elegies as the political state and internalized as ultimate sanctuary and part of the body, "spine in my spine." The mother herself is the "original garden," and later loves are seen as founded upon the first Edenic union between mother and child. Particularly in this collection, Valentine's God, unlike Wright's longed-for divine, is bodily invested, a God enwombed—or God as womb, as in "Ikon": "Swim in you, sleep / in you, let me, / Mother Lord" (*RW*, 7). The poem is a prayer, and the self is a cavity to be filled with spiritual intimation. Increasingly with *The Messenger* and with the new poems of her selected collection

Home Deep Blue, but most emphatically in *The River at Wolf*, her personae are endowed with a sense of God that is, as such, linguistically linked to the maternal: "Teacher, spine in my spine: / the spelling of the world / kneels down before the skate" (*RW*, 57).

"Seeing You" explicitly links the love of a mother, and the inheritance of a mother's fear and affection, with original knowledge and with later sexual relations. "That was the original garden: / seeing you" she writes of her mother (*RW*, 17). In part 2, "Lover," she echoes this assessment, now applied to a lover: "Oh that was the garden of abundance, seeing you" (*RW*, 18). Like the mother, the lover similarly reveals orality, fear, and benefi- cence. The poem unmistakably unites the experience of adult sexual love with the experience of love for a mother.

In "Butane," Valentine's speaker imagines an airship crashing and spark- ing fire, when suddenly a dwarf appears: "The dwarf says, *Hold it!* walking up between my legs / into my body: *I'd better see the fire skin*" (*RW*, 47). This disturbing poem images the mother initially as a hovering presence that, in death, must crash and cause further destruction. The dwarf would seem to be a surveyor of damage who enters the daughter's spiritual womb. In its puzzling compressions the poem intimates the manifold deaths experienced by this daughter. The death of the mother means the death of originary home (the womb) and symbolizes the speaker's own impending death; death becomes an inheritance delivered from the womb and its "fire skin." In the poem, the mother is linked to the genitals, and the self and the mother are symbolized as a burning airship. Valentine connects the mother to previous and future generations as the means of transmitting death as well as life. The daughter, a mother herself, must recognize her own position within this irrefutable chain of births and deaths.

In "At the Door" we operate with a reversed lens, for the daughter of the other poems is, in "At the Door," a mother. She sees herself in one moment of penetrating awareness as the maternal inhabiting a role that rays out beyond personal selfhood. The sense of self that the poem projects seems transparent as the white of an egg, a stretching gel covering but not occluding vision. In the poem the mother views her daughter in lamplight and recognizes that, for her daughter, the mother must fill in the imagina- tive and conceptual position of the maternal:

> It is not *I*,
> it is *Mother*,
> (But it is *I*.)

It is the first tableau, the first
red wellspring of *I*.

Through the mother as "wellspring," the child learns her own identity; through the child, the mother's experience of identity enlarges and radiates outward. The roles of mother and daughter overlap, even as the instinctual needs and desires that Valentine writes of are so basic as to seem animal-like:

Chimpanzee of longing,
outside the light,
wrap your long arms
around the globe of light,
hold your long haunches
wide open: be
ungodly I.

(*RW*, 53)

The expressed wish of the poem is for an all-encompassing embrace of such animal-like selves with their embarrassing, unboundaried reactions (the chimpanzee as a figure of longing, frenetic, ungainly, only mimicking the accepted social order). The mother longs to be human, "ungodly I," to return from ethereal spiritual realms and her preoccupation with mortality—as such, to be part of an antitranscendent earthly realm.

Valentine's speakers yearn for sanctuary, sought despite the ravages of alcoholism and sexual violence as these are coded in the poems as having occurred in earlier generations. In "Spring and Its Flowers" the first speaker, sounding as if prompted by a psychiatrist or a lover, imagines trading places with her partner in a tranquil fantasy. The poem's womblike Edenic moment is shattered, however, as the final lines deliver the rough shock that Valentine is often capable of delivering: "We didn't know / we were so close / to the world's mouth, the drunk bear's ashy thing" (*RW*, 2). The poem points to the terror of alcoholism, about which Valentine has spoken in interviews,[23] but also the threat of being devoured and sexually violated. The startling final image appears unboundaried: "the bear's thing," seemingly its sexual organ with all its vital suggestiveness, is modified by the sign of destruction: ash. As we move backward along the track of modifiers we see that drunkenness renders the bear as humanlike and shameful; here Valentine likens the overriding need for warmth and security, such womblike comfort, to addictive desires for fusion.

A central concern in this poetry revolves around the establishment of psychological boundaries between individuals, as the poems battle an impulse toward oblivion of self through absorption into another that mimics the preoedipal. Indeed, the raw strangeness of the poems emerges from the fact that they have not entirely acquiesced to the symbolic order. Selfhood at points is undifferentiated, and Valentine's doubles stand for undifferentiated feeling, a blurring in which feelings and sensations are not localized but spread across an environment. The challenge for this poet has been to preserve the sensitivity of this unboundaried self, its vulnerability, rather than to project an armored persona, a more stable force surely, but a persona less marked by psychic material.

Often Valentine writes of the desire for liberation from obsessive materials. Deliverance into something similar to an inspired spirituality distinguishes most of her more supple poems after *Pilgrims*. Valentine already revealed hers as a search for "the lightest lines" in her first collection's final poem, "To My Soul." Playing on her own name and in homage to the poetic examples of Emperor Hadrian and Pierre de Ronsard, she begins: "Scattered milkweed, valentine" (*DB*, 49). The scattering and dissolution of varied images and references toward self mark her poetics. Almost fifteen years after "To My Soul," she writes in "The Messenger," "Now I could scatter my body easily / if it was any use" (*M*, 28). Fragmentation and self-dissolution occur as notations on experience and suggest the momentary transformations into ephemerality that her speakers undergo. Identity as such is aerated or diffused. In times of psychic peril, Valentine's speakers experience themselves as unlocalized. In more positive, transformative moments, such ephemerality and self-scattering is transformed into a radiant diffuseness, lightly boundaried or outlined. No matter how seemingly open, such a sense of selfhood is not entirely permeable.

Over twenty years after "Dream Barker," Valentine returns to the desolation of that early poem, revising the meaning of its youthful dynamics in "Redemption." In the later poem she reconsiders the relationship between the woman and the man of "Dream Barker." She places her speaker in the territory of the earlier poem, with its underwater cave, the character Jim, and her memory of an abrupt departure, but, as we shall see, with an essential difference. The poem begins by noting that another poet "saw the word 'Confluence' in her sleep." The observation prompts Valentine's images of line and pattern as these emphasize discriminations, the telling details of difference: hair on a man's arm, a crease in a shoe. She then defines confluence as "two rivers joining, / or, the longing to return." She strikes again at what increasingly has come to be an important element of her work, a wish for ultimate union that takes its origins and its peculiar patterns from preoedipal experience:

> "Confluence": two rivers joining,
> or, the longing to return:
>
> because Jim, we parted
> on either side of this green island,
> Christ! it seems it was a hundred years ago.
>
> But now there is no inside wall:
> all down our bodies, from our heads to our feet,
> there's only a line like light,
> and all around us
> a line like an eggshell of light.
>
> (*RW,* 16)

Valentine's speaker moves from the purchased shell that was central to "Dream Barker" to the newly illuminated, spiritualized body, graphing the movement from matter to spirit. She remembers a past love relationship's destructiveness, but now she images boundaries as lines that resemble light, a psychological differentiation that is not coarsely defined but explicitly framed as luminous.

We might recall that in the early poem, "Dream Barker," the couple are separated after they decide to purchase a mysterious shell. Given the often negative link in Valentine's poems between false love and currency, a connection that becomes more clear after her first book, we can now see that the couple's attempt to buy the shell in "Dream Barker" is foredoomed. In Valentine's poems, purchases, even in dreams, are nullified or suggest a negative symbiosis, as she writes in a later poem: "This is / true desire, it lets you be. / It says, 'No money here'" (*RW,* 12). Similarly, in "My Mother's Body, My Professor, My Bower" she argues, "you can't protect yourself, / there is nothing to get" (*RW,* 46).

As we noted earlier, Valentine's poetry throughout her career takes much of its primary impetus from dreams. But her poetry has changed as her dreams have changed, enacting not only points of crisis but strategies for surviving deprivation. She transforms the bewilderments of abandonment into efforts toward individuation and a vision of relationship without possession of the other. Valentine's spiritual yearnings are salted with secular considerations, including the desire to return to a greater awareness of the body and, at moments, a liberation from either dependency or mastery over another, as in "The Free Abandonment Blues," a poem of self-acceptance. Her persona in this poem no longer is swayed by the demands of another, although she remembers clearly the temptation to succumb to such demands. She casts the one who gives love conditionally as a "blue-robed" mock priest. Rather than return his bid for binding relations, she turns, in the third stanza, to the same sort of saving potentials that she assumed at the time when she wrote *The Messenger*: nature, friendship, and sensuality without possessiveness. The voice that enters at the close of the poem advises patience. "Listen, it's only a little time longer to wait / When you have taken this path you need just a little more time to wait / Maybe not today the amazing loveliness but it won't be long for us to wait" (*RW*, 20). The poem moves from the present to the past to the future, concluding by anticipating "amazing loveliness."

As we have seen, Valentine has worked the tropes of abandonment through multiple dimensions. The woman who is left behind initially experiences the self as despised. In the course of midcareer Valentine then projects a psyche that moves beyond the individual ego. "I am trying to move into an other, into others" she told an interviewer, "to move out of the private self into an imagination of everyone's history, into the public world."[24] She accomplishes what amounts to a remarkable progression beyond the boundaries of the self without leaving behind a sense of the self's own interiority, the embattled private with its preoedipal trace memory. However lightened or emptied of expectation, such a provisional self nevertheless must learn to meet the embattled privacy of others.

4

The Master of the Masterless:
James Tate and the Pleasures of Error

James Tate does not seek control in origins or in art—nor in nature, in literary influence (with which he sports), or in environment, ancestry, or claims of expertise. Even the obscure predictability that some of Russell Edson's characters secure for themselves, at however gruesome a price, would seem impossible to obtain for Tate's speakers. They cannot effectively master phenomena; for them, all things are in the process of transformation, most pointedly themselves. Surely, as we shall see, Tate registers the dispiriting consequences of the dizzying multiplicity of contemporary life, yet at most moments—sometimes hard fast upon despair—he rides such currents of the vertiginous present to project freedom from self-consistency and self-control. Consider for a moment "Autosuggestion: USS North Carolina," a poem that directly signifies this ongoing process of establishing zones of psychic permissions through the perverse pleasure of articulating error and incompetence:

> . . . But what did we know?
> We were rank amateurs. We were poseurs of the worst sort.
> We were out of our league. We belonged in little league
> uniforms, but we couldn't afford them, and our sponsors
> were idiots and dunces and drifters and no-count
> amalgamated mud merchants. This left us free of debt
> and free of riches, which can be so heavy to transport.[1]

In a culture that has been devoted to ever-narrowing specializations of knowledge, Tate allows generative error to attain a welcome levity. To "not know" something hardly bothers his speakers—and may even prove emancipatory.

Tate presents our presumptions of mastery as suspect by dramatizing what he described in an interview as "the bizarre simultaneity of contemporary life."[2] As he has written in one poem, "We are breaking through so many illusions, / like some kind of ghost dance! / Nothing passes unmarked, / even the machines gossip."[3] His speakers engage in acts of ventriloquized authority, taking on only superficial rhetorical strategies of expertise as Tate assumes the flagrancy, the release of motion in language, a denunciation of classification as opposed to the abstract formalities of expertise. In doing so, he reveals our organizing structures as fictions that can be disrupted, paradoxically, by allowing the inexpert to assume the floor. His personae are without origin; mystery men, they are comical or despondent or, more properly, comical-despondent. And for these speakers there is no teleology. They engage in the desperate dance of the present where meaning will not be secured.

His speakers characterize themselves in a manner that emphasizes their inability to master their experiences: "I, a slave to a heap of cinders" (*SP,* 209); "I was the stuttering monster who accepted / his doom" (*SP,* 213); "Hello I am a cake of soap / dissolving in a warm bath" (*SP,* 101). Such personae puncture any possibility of the oracular; each is a man out of joint with his time but obstinately intent on the peculiarities of his circumstance and his invented roles. Tate gives us the emotional atmosphere of lives that have fallen short of conventional tests of legitimacy and good sense. In his poems the self as such is unabsorbed by traditional autobiography that would create the illusion of controlling representations of time and of establishing authorial consistency. Instead, his characters fail a proper self-writing. They pose in comic opposition to representations of self-aware, self-consistent, and responsible authority.

I wish to emphasize that I am not seeking to discover a gentle enervation in Tate's poems. In fact, I would like to suggest quite the opposite: that his poetry actively upends identities, retaining the curiousness of assuming selfhood, the perversity of the self to the self, including its shifting mood states and ineffective solutions. The actual work of the poems in their demasculinizing of male characters and caricaturing of heterosexual desires, in the voicing of need, weakness, and contingency, boldly counters patriarchal posturings of expertise.

As if to escape a culture's mandate for efficiency were success in itself, making for a free-floating sense of being, Tate aims at representations of failure with undisguised delight. Fred Miller Robinson describes comic tension in a way that may illuminate Tate: "The paradox of defeat and joy, destruction and creation, death and rebirth, must remain an unresolved paradox or we will lose the sense of the comic."[4] "Unresolved paradox" in Tate's poetry most clearly defies the totalizing strategy of cultural mastery. His poems are non-nostalgic, for the self is reimagined endlessly and detached from origins. The page, as such, is a space for practicing an avid sleight of hand in which identities are not assimilated and integrated so much as dispersed and shed. This profligacy with identities accounts for some of the excitement of his work. His explorers, tourists, and restless reckoners journey without discovering the source they ostensibly set out for; their fate is continual motion, which seems to be a good in and of itself for Tate, indicating a struggle against the petrification of sensibility and identity.

Given what he takes to be the vagaries of selfhood, for Tate autobiography is artifice that ought to be revealed as such. He does not reject clichés of autobiography, the already-made, so much as use them as launchpads for further investigations of new language contexts. In "Intimidations of an Autobiography" the speaker points to the very artificiality of autobiography—and his sense of being initially defeated by its claims before reasserting his own aesthetic of self-dismantling:

> . . . I arrange the day
> for you. I stop and say,
> you would not believe how happy
>
> I was as a child,
> to some logs.
>
> (*SP*, 17)

Taking his notes on current place and remembered childhood—with a countenance suddenly effaced—the musing quasi-autobiographer in this poem finally summons the dubious cliché, "I'm calling the cows home" (*SP*, 18). In other poems that test the limits of autobiography, Tate makes many selves, including fractured selves, and even suddenly expunged selves, exposing the conventions of traditional autobiography as inadequate to his sense of identity as not only multiple but in constant transformation. He would celebrate the power to enter other identities and to retreat from them. In "Tragedy Comes to the Bad Lands" Tate embeds his own name in the poem as a mythical Tate (somewhat like Wright's mythical Charles) framed against a historical backdrop as a comic sufferer:

> . . . Look! I implore, who's
> sashaying across the Bad
> Lands now—it's trepid riding
> Tate (gone loco in the
> cabeza) out of his little
> civilized element—Oh!
> It's bound to end in tears.
>
> (*SP,* 26)

He takes pleasure in this self-effacement; the hysteria of what seems suddenly a voice-over duplicates some elements of the hounded pathos of much conventional autobiographical narrative. His characters are at the mercy of the passage of time and dread the reversion into the past that autobiography stabilizes. Time is solidified as a place, a domestic space, and the poems center on the anxiety of reversion. In "Time X" Tate plays with a brand name of watch and an appellation for a view of time: time as the crossed-out star, as the unknown, as the ineffable, as an absence, a forbidden essence, and a blocked exit. "But for now his clock has stopped watching, / his back-up band is dead" (*SP,* 172).

He would find a more wholly physical inebriation of sorts in the curious prose poem "Waking" with its voluptuously surreal comedy. In this prose poem a man is halved in an odd bath, split between the world of waking and dream. In manic compressions Tate disavows the standard rhetorical consistency that deepens toward tragic denouement:

> I dried myself vigorously. Then, with considerable strain, I lifted the tortoise-shell comb which had grown enormous overnight, to my head perched high on the flagpole of my neck. If I'd had any hair left the crush of the comb might have been softened. As it was, I was split perfectly down the middle, nose, navel and penis in equal servings. I felt like a deer chasing a mirage.
>
> There was a taste of honey on the razor blade, honey that sucks bees.
>
> (*SP,* 133)

This speaker experiences the realm between dream and full consciousness as a location of self-inflicted violence (however absurd), as if to suggest that what is done to the man in his bath is what Tate would do to any culturally sanctioned sources of meaning; he would bathe meaning, including our perception of time's passage, in comic force, actively dividing our stubborn fictions of the unitary self.

As these brief examples suggest, at times Tate's poems seem to be the productions of an inventive loner deliriously at work to create his scenarios from the most banal materials: grooming, waking, and daydreams. Representing an almost cinematic speed of sensation, Tate's poems take the insults and exhilarations of contemporary culture as their most engaging source. The banal that we are presumably to control in daily life proves, if not entirely uncontrollable as in Edson's poems, to be possessed of near-demonic force. That is, in his poems the banal *asserts* itself. In early career, Tate saw boredom as a cultural defense, a form of repression—and poetic capital. The early poem "It's Not the Heat So Much as the Humidity" (*SP,* 58) makes vivid the mundane, as objects collide or threaten to merge with similar objects. The cliché from which the poem springs suggests a wilting of language so pervasive that neither the manic search for celebrity nor the pursuit of innovation can provide relief. The ennui of the "sexually active people in Westport" ("The Chaste Stranger"), the proliferating code words for nuclear devastation that suggest inane indifference to ultimate tragedy ("Smart and Final Iris"), the stupendous boredom that characterizes a city ("The Wheelchair Butterfly): in such cases, Tate experiments with exhausted linguistic structures and invests in dizzyingly inventive assaults on language formulae.

Tate published his first book in 1967, in the near wake of the confessional poets and in the midst of the resurgence of neosurrealists. His poems suggest both legacies. That is, we have in his poems the focus on self and self-display of the confessionals combined with the velocity, unpredictability, and unexpected juxtapositions of the surreal. Speaking of critics' perceptions of him as a surrealist, Tate has noted that the surrealist worldview appears inescapable to him. "I don't know why everyone goes around acting like it's strange. Just thumb through any magazine, look at any advertisement on television. That's obviously a successful movement. It's taken over the world."[5] As John Ashbery noted in the citation for the Tanning Prize that Tate was awarded, Tate "refute[s] the idea of Surrealism as something remote from daily experience, a hermetic art for a privileged few." For Tate, "Surrealism is something very like the air we breathe, the unconscious mind erupting in one-on-one engagements with the life we all live, every day."[6] Surrealism for Tate is a given, and his poems actively compete with the surreal realities of daily life.

Like surrealism as Tate describes it, in some ways the confessional poets' legacy has been absorbed culturally as well. The "substance" of some confessions by Lowell, Sexton, and Plath may appear almost quaint in comparison to the quasi-therapeutic elements of television talk shows and tabloids—and even the aura surrounding political elections as candidates reflect on their personal pasts. Pointedly, in Tate's poems there is no urge to confess; the self is far too wily and unstable. Its "confessions" outpace conceptions of the centrality of the self. His characters do not pretend to sincerity. They seldom confess deeds as much as they propel before us diffuse states of mind.

Attempts to link Tate to the deep imagists have been less convincing than acknowledgments of his debt to surrealism and the confessional poets. Paul Breslin, wrongly it seems to me, links Tate to deep-image poetry, a poetry that "comes from a source beyond the socialized self, far away from the prosaic doings of our daylit lives among others."[7] On the contrary, I would argue, Tate is keenly focused on patterns of shared language and the prerogatives of culture. The unconscious is not drawn into hermetically in his poems; rather, Tate reveals the mind's stuttering flashes upon outward circumstances. When Tate writes directly in terms of the poetic of Charles Simic, his contemporary, a poet with whom he has been compared and who writes more clearly with debts to deep imagists, he does so with parodistic intent. In "A Guide to the Stone Age" (dedicated to Simic), Tate affectionately lampoons the deep-image poem and its hieroglyphics of the primordial self (*SP*, 100). When a second, questioning speaker enters the poem, the "elemental" energies of the scene are vented. That is, Tate allows dialectics to alter the original deep-imagist pattern. He distances himself from the portentousness of parts of Simic's poetic in favor of his own poetic: speculative, self-conscious, multidirectional, and suspicious of mystification. In miniature, Tate's strategy in "A Guide to the Stone Age" points to the write-overs and reinscriptions of his earlier lines in much of his own work; he interrogates not only other sensibilities but the initial style and sensibility that he has erected in each of his poems. The deflations that he works on other poetics are even more often aimed at his own first impulses in individual poems as he constructs subsequent lines.

Tate's homages to other writers tend toward the playful and involve a literalizing of language formulae reminiscent of Edson—as if a ludic spirit were a necessary defense against poetic influence, and as if he would unmaster his masters. He also manages to gesture toward continuities that he has inherited from predecessors. His twelfth book, *Worshipful Company of Fletchers*, opens with an epigraph from Emily Dickinson: "I always ran Home to Awe when a child, if anything befell me. He was an awful Mother, but I liked him better than none." The quotation underlines Tate's own quirkily singular family romance, the tweaking of the mundane actual in the vicinity of the awe-full. "Home" is awe: the state of mystery and of interior space, of inner reverie, that his poems frequently circle about seems rooted in Dickinson's similar preoccupations.

His tendency to absorb other aesthetics may be seen more clearly in his debt to the poems of Wallace Stevens. His fidelity to the play of the imagination is similar to Stevens's, and Tate himself has acknowledged an affinity with his modernist predecessor, based on what he calls a similar "density of imagery" and the fact that both poets create highly colored projections of imagination. In his effort to "exhibit a way of seeing"—Tate's self-description of his poetry—he echoes Stevens's efforts. Surely an early piece by Tate, "Poem" ("High in the Hollywood Hills a door opens"), to cite one obvious instance, suggests in its extravagant verbal play and descriptions of weather and place similar elements in the poetry of Stevens. Yet unlike Stevens, Tate is a poet of readier identifications between his speakers and others. In "Poem" dream and reality intermingle and "the word, // [is] itself a dream." The speaker watches a Chinese girl swimming in a pool, yet the sensory floribunda and the call to "reality," to the actual girl, are supplanted by his imagination. The man dances alone without having met the girl, and desire itself is experienced as a strong call, but the supposed aftereffects of this not-quite-encounter between the man and the girl are pitifully inadequate. "The souvenir ashtray" holds, after all, the waste of "the good cigar." That the scene takes place "high in the Hollywood Hills" (*SP,* 37) refers us to our modern mecca of illusion and reinforces our sense of the fictive quality of the search for a part of reality that will satisfy the desirous imagination. Yet neither reality nor imagination saves Tate's speaker. Like one of the elders who desires Susanna, another bathing woman whom Stevens so famously conjured, Tate's persona finds that the reality of this particular woman evades him, and he is lifted into the artifice of his imagination, which, in itself, cannot entirely meet his needs.

Tate's is not an urban sensibility, although the tone of insouciance that he sometimes adopts suggests Frank O'Hara's urban poetry. Neither is he a poet who takes the natural world as unmediated, nor is he wont to invest the natural world with sacred meaning. The natural cannot serve him as origin precisely because it is corrupted by the tracemarks of human ambition. Nature is written over with human desire and human invention; it is occluded by not only technology but by human speech: "The mountains

had long ago crumbled away, / erased by some soft artillery on the radio"
(*SP,* 191). He positions the self as an avatar of an exquisite, but confusing, in
fact nearly disabling, sensitivity to linguistic impressions more often than to
nature. Human life is a quirky error inflamed by unappeasable appetites:
"Typos in a U-boat, we were all members / of Nature's alphabet. But we
wanted more" (*SP,* 171). In "Nausea, Coincidence," a wasp, as harbinger
from the natural world, is comically attacked and made the hapless sign of
sentimental poetry: "I pop him a good pop, insert the corpse into a volume
of love poems" (*SP,* 196). The man who speaks in "In My Own Backyard"
catalogs his lawn, its trees and bushes, its chicken coop, its compost heap,
and its proximity to neighbors, measuring the limits of his property and the
limits of his subject matter as reflected within an inner life that cannot entirely ground itself:

> I grab my throat and wrestle me to the ground.
> "There, there," I say, "lighten up ol' boy."
> "It's a free country, it's your own backyard."
> I listen intently: sky and daisies burlesque each other,
>
> bivouacked between worlds.

(*WCF,* 69)

The poem is refracted through a persona's psychic woundedness marked
by comic self-denigration. Here the stance toward the self is not that of
ecstatic or melancholy self-reverie. When melancholy threatens to invade
Tate's poems, our expectations are most often thwarted. The persona then
divides in half (an action taken in the prose poem "Waking"), committing a
quirkily comic self-violation, counseling himself through a cliché that takes
on a mordant twist: "lighten up ol' boy." A second cliché widens the appli-
cability of the poem; the backyard is "a free country" even though its con-
glomeration of decay and memory reflect disassociated being.

Tate's commitment to rupturing conventions of optimal performance
and self-consistency has not been achieved without inciting critical puzzle-
ment. Vendler has described Tate's poems as "misanthropic."[8] James Finn
Cotter sees Tate as "too cunning and whimsical."[9] William Logan finds in
the poetry "an acknowledgement of failure, a suggestion that nothing, not
even surrealism, will work as a method any longer, even that language, or
communication . . . has become impossible."[10] Such analyses of an overall

"chill" neglect disruptive pleasures that make Tate's poetry both seductive and resistant to critical appropriation, as this poet enacts the failure of authority, including critical authority, through skewed juxtapositions, transfigured clichés, and proclamations of the wholly inadequate response. Amidst subverted cause and effect, flux and baffling multiplicity, Tate denies presumptions of control in ways that make his works an enlivening force in contemporary poetry. As Lyotard well over a decade ago informed us: "Postmodern knowledge is not simply a tool of the authorities; it refines our sensitivity to differences and reinforces our ability to tolerate the incommensurable. Its principle is not the expert's homology, but the inventor's paralogy."[11] Of course, Tate has never been a comfortable poet to read, for he is engaged in tests of reading conventions; his "inventor's paralogy" has always risked disparagement aimed at not only his speakers but at the earnest reader. Certainly it is possible to find in Tate an ambivalence toward his readers: "half hating you, / half eaten by the moon" (*SP,* 65). At times, his reader/listener is portrayed as dead or deadened, absent, or inanimate. In some poems his hostility spills over into comic-sadistic recipes and chants. Such catalogs follow a slippery slope from poor consequences to the hardly imaginable, turning to mock terror as in "Sleep" and "First Lesson." In "Yellow Newspaper and a Wooden Leg" he comments surreptitiously on the poet's anxiety in the face of the reader's avid hunger for absolute meaning. In the poem, a group of children gaze into a crematorium window. On one level, a predictable trope juxtaposes death with birth, for the children peering into the crematorium are "baby chicks," "in the full bloom of their delivery." On another level, the poem addresses the poet's relationship with the reader who waits for the immolation of the work, the "combustion" of the poem's meaning within the reader's mind:

> . . . the corpse yawned,
> for a moment sat up. Then, plunging, it seethed
> and disappointed, finally cringed hugging itself
> blood to ashes, and to a precise, metallic aroma.

> (*SP,* 198)

Like the desirous reader, the children expect a legend, a fortune of meaning, a legendary exit, but the corpse (or the corpus of work) collapses into ash, into an odor rather than a visible and substantial presence. While Tate invests in such taunts directed at the reader, he also implicates his own persona in this gamesmanship, as if language inevitably were to manhandle all who enter its borders. And just as the reader is, in a sense, the perpetual amateur in regard to the poem, Tate often allies himself closely with the amateur's position, testing his own authority as maker and reader of texts. Indeed, here lies one of the defining paradoxes of his work; while Tate is a "master" of poetry, one of the most distinctive and inventive poets of his generation, he writes often and with greatest affection of the amateur, the pointedly inexpert. By presenting portraits of ineffective, baffled, and histrionic amateurs, he refuses to impersonate authority but revels in presenting linguistic and behavioral errors, in "mismanaging" reality.

Tate's poems foregrounding ancestry, the authority of the past, and the authority of identity (that which is defined, determined, conscious) are particularly revealing. He attempts to deflate traditional assumptions of even the possibility of mastering phenomena. Other symptomatic poems are those which focus on beginnings and beginners, most notably children or childlike personae, or on frustrated attempts at arrival or at closure, that is, on situations or persons characterized by the absence of certainty and authority.

In brief form, one way in which Tate appropriates assumptions of mastery is through casting founding fictions—fictions of origin—as charmingly inept narratives. In "My Great Great Etc. Uncle Patrick Henry" a family proves to be a comically disappointing institution as, ironically, the name of the patriot neutralizes their discussion:

> There's a fortune to be made in just about everything
> in this country, somebody's father had to invent
> everything—baby food, tractors, rat poisoning.
> My family's obviously done nothing since the beginning
> of time. They invented poverty and bad taste
> and getting by and taking it from the boss.
> O my mother goes around chewing her nails and
> spitting them in a jar: You shouldn't be ashamed
> of yourself she says, think of your family.
> My family I say what have they ever done but
> paint by numbers the most absurd and disgusting scenes
> of plastic squalor and human degradation.
> Well then think of your great great etc. Uncle
> Patrick Henry.
>
> (*SP*, 116)

Comically, the poem dramatizes a battle between a mother and a son for supremacy in determining family fictions. The son, after all, has assumed for his family the "authority" of absolute failure. Among the family's inventions, "getting by and taking it from the boss" serves as evidence of their submission to present authority. Submission to the past does them no more good. Yet in the son's conception, his forebears prove to be the founders of failure. Such absolute failure, however, is yet another presumption; the son would totalize the family and its origins. The assertion of complete failure is itself a move toward mastery of the past and a disguised strategy for counterdominance. And the mother's attempt to dissolve her son's fiction through the name of Patrick Henry fails in turn, for her retaliation is absurd and sententious. Both conceptions of absolute mastery and of absolute failure, Tate insinuates, may be enthralling structures.

Just as the name of Patrick Henry cannot solve this family crisis, nomenclature in this poetry points to the impossibility of retrieving a final truth or discovering an ultimate master. Of course, names place us in culture and make clear the first submission of the human being to the dictates of language. In Tate's poems, names emphasize the inadequacy of their bearers. Alfonse Lackluster, Slim Victual, Bunny, Snorpa Little-Dew, Opening Valves—to bleat such names in the midst of crisis is to announce futility; the supposed rescuer is already a caricature of incapacity. In similar fashion, the titles of Tate's collections suggest ineptitude. *The Lost Pilot* signals defeat. *The Oblivion Ha-Ha, Hints to Pilgrims,* and *Absences* explicitly refer to baffled travelers and foiled entrances. Other titles—*Riven Doggeries, Constant Defender*—call up embattled and farcical personae, as if the very conception of identity proved an inherently hapless one.

Names are explored further in "Tell Them   Was Here." The open space within the title alerts us to the self as blank space, signaling both nonidentity and, conversely, a self's freedom from linguistic categories. The speaker of the poem may be a ghost to himself and to others. At any rate, his isolation could hardly be more complete. "No one was home," for his ancestors apparently have abandoned this figure:

> I got there on time
> and no one was home.
> I waited, paced the sidewalk.
>
> . . . .
>
> *Unreliable ancestors!*
> Then it was night and I began
> to doubt: It's all lies,

> I came from no one, nowhere,
> had no folks and no hometown,
>
> no old friends. I was born
> of rumors, a whisper in one
> state, an unsubstantiated brawl
> in another, uncontiguous state.
>
> Green was here, I scrawled
> on a scrap of paper, and stuck it
> inside the screen. Started to leave,
>
> turned, scratched out my name—
> then wrote it back again.
>
> (*SP*, 188)

The self within the poem, rumor-made and as such composed of language, gives his name as "Green," a descriptive, including a descriptive of innocence and naiveté, not a substance. Both the speaker's origin and his identity are "unsubstantiated." Yet he holds out the bare hope of being only temporarily deserted, as his final actions suggests. That is, he hasn't even the certainty of absolute abandonment. Perhaps someone will return to the house after he has left. His actions—scribbling his name, scratching it out, writing it again over the scratched-out name—create a palimpsest in which his identity bears the marks of a reinscription, as if any identity he could hope for must be predicated on a partial erasure and a rewriting that reflects his second thoughts, his half-illegible self-inscription. While names are normally granted authority in culture, signaling a certain and continuous identity, in Tate they are used disruptively, violating expectations of psychological consistency. Names in this poetry do not reveal stable or singular identities, and personae are compelled to doubt even their parentage.

Journeys without destinations, the expected arrivals that do not materialize: these reappear with remarkable frequency in Tate's poetry. The title poem of his first book, *The Lost Pilot*, is dedicated to Tate's father, a World War II pilot who died in action when his plane was shot down in 1944 during the poet's infancy. The image of "compulsive orbiting," the circularity that afflicts so many of Tate's characters, is inscribed in the title of Tate's first collection and in the title poem's plot and images. In like fashion, his syntactical "orbiting" in much of his poetry, through thematic digression and unexpected shifts in speech registers, reflects his choice to extend upon the fate of not only his father but his culture. Any cultural collapse of meaning is doubly pressured in Tate's poems by his earliest circumstances, inflected as they were by his father's death.

The insistence on escaping identity that we have noted in these poems is prefigured in "The Lost Pilot." While for Edson, faces are often blank ciphers, and for Valentine they may be light-filled, radiant vessels, for Tate the face, recognition of which most often defines identity in culture, is an enigmatic mask. In the "Lost Pilot" a repeated turn on the word *face* leaves us with the lost pilot as an ever-absent divine, "a tiny, African god" (*SP,* 16) who has left the son an earth-bound supplicant. The father's face "grew dark, / and hard like ebony." It is this iconic face that the son imagines and wishes to touch: "I would touch you, / read your face. . . . // I would touch your face as a disinterested // scholar touches an original page" (*SP,* 15). To attain a vision of such a father's face is to trade places with the dead, without separate or articulated existence. The son's own ignorance of his father nearly dooms him to self-diminishment, collapsing his ability to attain a mature psychic life. In the newly quiet and resigned tenor of the poem's last lines, the fatherless son asserts of his father and himself, "misfortune / placed these worlds in us" (*SP,* 16). The suggestion of placement and causation is significant. The worlds *in* his protagonist (circling, splitting, wobbling, shrinking, bursting with a pantheon of unfortunates) animate his poems. "I hear a laugh swim up / from the part of myself / I've killed" (*SP,* 102), he writes in another poem, and yet the sense of "undead" activity lends curious vitality to his work as Tate deals with seemingly indestructible psychic material.

The speaker who inhabits a number of these poems may be exempted, as I have suggested, from some patriarchal presumptions of authority and continuity. Such characters are freed from mythologies of dominance and self-consistency. And yet in early career one senses Tate's ambivalence regarding mythologies of masculinity. As Mark Jarman observes of "The Lost Pilot," written in the 1960s, the death of Tate's father, the central character of the title poem, "symbolized the gulf between generations during that vivid decade [the 1960s]."[12] In "The Initiation" this deadening by osmosis occurs as if the death of Tate's father's were, again, the son's, as the poem registers inchoate loss:

> The jowl of the dead
> is agape with infinite abandon
> as if he were about to sing:

> if we concentrate
> he may remember the words.
>
> (*SP,* 49)

In "Deadlines" Tate sees the manic intensity of his own sensibility as both an affront to and a temptation to unnamed, destructive impulses:

> He puts the dead one down, walks around of course of course in circle in circle he walks around in circles of course of course in circle. I killed the dead one and now of course of course I am going to kill that crazy live one.
>
> (*SP,* 134)

The loss of patriarchal presumption is not simply gleefully met in Tate, but at points in his early body of work it is viewed with ambivalence. In consequence, the comedy of his work is deepened by his peculiarly mixed feelings.

Through "The List of Famous Hats" Tate posits a failed attempt at mastery in a manner that may complicate our observations. In the prose poem, Napoleon is conjured by virtue of his name and a few physical signs, but the prose poem intimates that there is no "bottom" to fictions of mastery; they are infinitely capricious. Napoleon is made comically monstrous, described by a folk theoretician of sorts whose brief dissertation on Napoleon's hat is, finally, a description of power. Hats, of course, may be conceived of as "second heads," and the hat here represents authority as a symbol of both grand design and empire:

> Napoleon's hat is an obvious choice I guess to list as a famous hat, but that's not the hat I have in mind. That was his hat for show. I am thinking of his private bathing cap, which in all honesty wasn't much different than the one any jerk might buy at a corner drugstore now, except for two minor eccentricities. The first one isn't even funny: Simply it was a white rubber bathing cap, but too small. Napoleon led such a hectic life ever since his childhood, even farther back than that, that he never had a chance to buy a new bathing cap and still as a grown-up—well, he didn't really grow that much, but his head did: He was a pinhead at birth, and he used, until his death really, the same little tiny bathing cap that he was born in, and this meant that later it was very painful to him and gave him many headaches, as if he needed more. So, he had to vaseline his skull like crazy to even get the thing on. The second eccentricity was that it was a

tricorn bathing cap. Scholars like to make a lot out of this, and it would be easy to do. My theory is simple-minded to be sure: that beneath his public head there was another head and it was a pyramid or something.

(*SP*, 225)

Through repeated qualifications, this speaker duplicates the rhetorical strategies of academic discourse. Indeed, he seems to be an inept cousin to the literary critic who would search through the text for the "second head" of an innate authority. Certainly, authority may thrive through mystification, protecting itself by making glamorous mysteries of its processes. Yet the pose of Napoleon, as decoded by the speaker in this depiction, is anything but glamorous. Instead, the private is represented by a bathing cap, the sort "any jerk might buy at a corner drugstore." The cap's "eccentricities" (it is too small and shaped like a tricorn) play off popular conceptions of Napoleon through two signs of the historical figure: his physical stature and his attire. As he constructs his theory, Tate's speaker builds toward a preposterous invention: "beneath his public head there was another head and it was a pyramid or something." And yet, since a pyramid is a structure in which other structures reside, might the head reveal yet other heads, other antechambers of authority, "or something"? The very imprecision of Tate's final phrase accents the uncertain and "simple-minded" delights of his speaker. This speaker might infinitely delay our arrival toward any knowledge of what is beneath Napoleon's head and, in consequence, beneath the elaborate outward vestiges of authority. Tate's speaker overturns not only the iconic authority of Napoleon but his own authority.

In this context, Roland Barthes's exploration of the authority of a speaker "in a teaching situation" illuminates Tate's strategy of presenting an "imperfect orator":

[T]he speaker is bothered by all this Law that the act of speaking is going to introduce into what he wants to say, . . . he uses the irreversibility of speech in order to disturb its legality: correcting, adding, wavering, the speaker moves into the infinitude of language, superimposes on the simple message that everyone expects of him a new message that ruins the very idea of a message and, through the shifting reflection of the blemishes and excesses with which he accompanies the line of the discourse, asks us to believe with him that language is not to be reduced to communication. By all these operations, which come near the wavering movement of the Text, the imperfect orator hopes to render less disagreeable the role that makes every speaker a kind of policeman.

Such an attempt to "speak badly" may create yet another role, Barthes
notes: that of "a master who is human, too human—*liberal.*" What is to be
done? "Nothing [is] is to be done: language is always a matter of force, to
speak is to exercise a will to power; in the realm of speech, there is no
innocence, no safety."[13] Tate's response is to present speakers who are inexpert and yet exuberant, displacing heads and names as a way at least temporarily to displace positions and law. Masteries of fact and event are swept
aside. This poet's answer to authority is to present the inept and the
softheaded—and to allow revelry in the pleasures of inventive error.

In "Goodtime Jesus" the position of "the Law" as the father, here the
godly father, is deflated by Tate's projection of Jesus as an errant son of the
Law. Tate's Jesus is humanly banal. He dreams of deathly creatures (a vision suspiciously like hell), and oversleeps:

> Jesus got up one day a little later than usual. He had been dreaming so
> deep there was nothing left in his head. What was it? A nightmare, dead
> bodies walking all around him, eyes rolled back, skin falling off. But he
> wasn't afraid of that. It was a beautiful day. How 'bout some coffee? Don't
> mind if I do. Take a little ride on my donkey, I love that donkey. Hell, I
> love everybody.
>
> (*SP,* 177)

Goodtime Jesus need not fear hellish dreams. As the divine he might visit
hell, but he surely won't have to live there. Bonded to a donkey, this figure is
naive, affectionate, and empty-headed: "there was nothing left in his head."
He is crossed between nightly horror and daily pleasantries. And through
the paradox of "Hell, I love everybody," with its juxtaposition of uncritical
affection and eternal punishment, Tate forces the affable and the tragic to
coincide, an uneasy combination that he finds particularly revealing in terms
of contemporary sensibilities. The son of God, usually a sign of law, is here
a creature oriented toward pleasure. And here, too, is the allure of the un-
qualified statement. Masters, after all, do not love everybody; masters dis-
criminate and create final judgments.

In a later poem, "The Expert," Tate speaks more overtly about the
authority who has attained cultural legitimacy, and he displays irritation
toward the outward confidence of the assumed expert. While, as we have
observed, Tate criticizes political mystification as a means of gaining power
over others, at the same time "The Expert" attains some of its human and
defiant dignity—however humorous—from Tate's belief in the private sen-

sibility, as if his poetry seriously suggests that "beneath [our] head there is another head" (as in his prose poem on Napoleon). He intimates that despite its efforts to disguise itself, authority is underlaid with human imperfections and human unpredictability. What I am suggesting is that while Tate interrogates authority's mystification of its own processes in public institutions, his poetry finally defends the actual unknowability of the complete human being. The speaker focusing on his curiosity about Napoleon suggests that there is more to us than our "public head." The man who claims expertise about phenomena, as in "The Expert," is influenced as well by his intense subjectivity. Indeed, it is a recognition of intense subjectivity that Tate proposes as a defense against the predations of mastery— including our own fantasies of absolute self-mastery. "Who among us / invited this expert?" he asks.

> We have no idea what he has given
> his life for, though I think
> it has something to do with
> a monster under the bed.
> He is growing old before our eyes,
> and no one can catch him now,
> no one, that is, except his lost mother.[14]

In this examination of assumed expertise, the demons of childhood, the loss of a mother, and the threat of regression underlie apparent expertise. Tate is often a Freudian at heart; the links in his chain of suffering go back to childhood, and it is childhood's dependency and vulnerability, even its terror, that he fixes on. The expert mounts his evidence, for Tate, above an abyss of primitive need.

If for Tate our "unreliable ancestors" and the language we use to describe the past are questionable, so too is place—place as a determinant of personal identity (that which endows the developing human identity with its "sense of place"), and as a goal, as destination. Like Green of "Tell Them   Was Here," other personae exhibit uneasy relationships to their surroundings. In *Viper Jazz* Tate titles a poem "Once I Was Young in the Land of Baloney,"[15] a comic announcement of falsification; baloney is not only pretense ("No matter how you slice it," Carl Sandburg told us, "it's still baloney"), it connotes nonsense. Satisfactory meaning cannot be found in accounts of our historical origins; nor does the play of

language offer arrival at any place signifying substantial identity: "No matter how far he might travel / his secret story is written somewhere, / in
the generous air, in the distance" (*VJ,* 18). In the contingent sphere of these
poems, destinations inevitably prove shifting or illusory. "I who have no
home have no destination either," Tate's speaker declares in "The Boy."[16]
Among the most common figures in this poetry are wanderers, awkward
tourists who remain puzzled by their surroundings. "I'm forced to con-
clude *keep walking, / what's at the core of it, keep walking*" (*SP,* 174). In alien and
baffling landscapes Tate's speakers repeatedly acknowledge their errant
homing instincts and prove to be connoisseurs of their own inadequacies:
"Let profit be / the love we part with, and failure / the first day of the rest
of our lives."[17]

Repeatedly, journeys may not be mastered; Tate's speakers discover
that they falter upon their arrival. As in "The Chaste Stranger," his travelers find themselves "whirling in a spangled frenzy toward / a riddle and a
doom" (*SP,* 230). "The Wild Cheese," for instance, presents an arrival that
parallels Tate's explorations of names and places through its focus on a
central figure's ultimate end. Just as Tate's conclusions do not generally
absorb his poem's multiple energies, so, too, no final homecoming awaits to
clarify and resolve the dilemma of the wild cheese. And while the name of
Jesus serves as a displacement for the name of the Law or the Word, so too,
the cheese in this poem is placed in a position in which we expect, because
of the genre that the poem parodies, an identity of some sort to appear, no
matter how veiled in mystery. Like so many of Tate's inventions, the cheese
is a vulnerable loner of unknown origin who cannot "know his place" and
is set upon in a hostile environment:

>Small snarling boys ran
>circles around it;
>and just as they began
>throwing stones, the Mayor
>appeared and dispersed them.
>
>He took the poor ignorant
>head of cheese home,
>and his wife scrubbed it
>all afternoon before
>cutting it with a knife
>and serving it after dinner.

> The guests were delighted
> and exclaimed far into the night,
> "That certainly was a wild cheese!"
>
> (*SP*, 185)

Cleverly, Tate draws upon the Western with its common episode: a stranger arrives in town. His stranger is taken into protection, however, only to be betrayed and destroyed. He is eaten—the outcome, of course, that one expects for cheese, and a fate that prompts empty conversation: "That certainly was a wild cheese!" The poem subverts the standard narrative plot of rescue, for no savior arrives. Nor does the loner through skill, wit, or courage save himself. And this is hardly a wild cheese, with connotations of savage freedom, but one easily consumed. The head of cheese, the head of Napoleon, the empty head of Goodtime Jesus: Tate's poems are marked by a consciousness of heads as symbols of mastery, but here, mastery that inevitably falters.

While Tate prefers to eschew the fixity of closure in his poems, he is deeply interested in beginnings. Beginnings, whether within tales about neophytes or through our own efforts as readers within poems that call for our retracing, our recapitulating the act of beginning, allow him to disturb assumptions of authority. Edward Said informs us: "Beginning is not only a kind of action; it is also a frame of mind, a kind of work, an attitude, a consciousness":[18]

> What are the conditions that allow us to call something a beginning? First of all, there must be the desire, the will, and the true freedom to reverse oneself, to accept thereby the risks of rupture and discontinuity: for whether one looks to see where and when he began, or whether he looks in order to begin now, he cannot continue as he is.[19]

Such experiences of "rupture and discontinuity" distinguish Tate's poetry. "This strand of dark beginnings I call my only friend"[20] proves, for Tate, to be the poem itself. As such, Tate's preoccupation with mastery is fruitfully complicated, and authority in its relation to author is brought to crisis as he avoids a steady point of view for his narrators. His affection for fracturing logical sequence and for breaking with tonal consistency further complicates any perspective on the author as textual authority.

In considering this poet's explorations of failure, his fascination with children becomes clearer, for children as initiates, "beginners" in existence, serve to counteract images of cultural authority. Paul Smith, writing of

Barthes on failure, suggests that "the writer, in order to decompose the great structures under which we live in thrall, may have to learn to speak childishly, to prolong the fragmentary sensations of *jouissance*, valorize the subject's irremediable division."[21] As yet undomesticated by cultural ideology, Tate's children are innocents whom stimuli overwhelm, and their "irremediable divisions" are made manifest. "Poem for the Sandman," for instance, figures the unsettling terrain of childhood:

> The child begins to walk
> toward her own private sleeping place.
> In the pocket of her bathrobe
> she clinches a hand grenade.
> She is lumbering through the lumberyard
> like a titmouse with goosebumps.

Even the sandman, presented here as somewhat like a drug dealer, cannot be trusted. Stepping from the pinball hall to "mend her cocoon, to rinse her shroud" (*SP*, 182), he promises a fix of sorts that would temporarily insulate the child from suffering. Sleep, a neutral province overseen by this boss, may only briefly soothe the child. Those who master others seldom protect in the world of these poems; at best they anaesthetize. And here is a bedtime story in which our heroine's destination is sleep as a brief respite from yet "another war" of painful consciousness and cultural mayhem.

Similarly, at the center of "Nobody's Business," a child's drama has the quality of an eerily effective, outsized cartoon, each moment writ large in response to an intolerable anxiety that magnifies perception. Tate once again depicts ancestors, the supposed founders of meaning, as incapable of governing meaning—whether in terms of origins or identity. The poem frames the scene of another unsuccessful arrival, this one witnessed by a child:

> On its nail an apron flapped, then froze.
> And in the hallway, slippers fidgeted, then stood
> dazed like questionable theatrical props
> on the stairs. A suitcase wiped its brow:
> So this is the last stop and no one
> is here to meet me.

(*SP*, 186)

"A child with his birthday telescope"—the child in the mother's womb or in the womblike conditions of infancy—"has observed all this," Tate writes.

As the poem continues, all action slows for the child's imminent "birth," his realization of both his own mortality and his "untouchable" isolation:

> . . . He tells no one,
> it is nobody's business. But nothing is forgotten.
> Clad only in fluid intervals, he is untouchable,
> mincing toward that housewarming
> that is surely his.
>
> *(SP,* 187)

"It is nobody's business." This child guards his mystery, bearing his own knowledge ("nothing is forgotten"). Tate's title echoes the child's defensive posture; this is pointedly nobody's business. The scene the child observes is marked by absence, by the arrival of *no body.* The traveler who cannot arrive is a nobody, a "no body," the contemporary Odysseus, who unlike the ancient Odysseus does not return. As in so many of Tate's poems, homecoming itself is perpetually "halted in mid-flight." In spite of his persona's ardent desires, what has begun cannot be concluded and as such mastered. The father of meaning, the master ancestor who would redeem traditional structure of coherent identity and consistent authority, will not put in an appearance for both Tate's innocents and his incompetents.

Tate makes of the powerless either the messengers of stark terror or, in other venues, when the inexpert speak, the bearers of unexpected happiness, the soft attenuated happiness of a solitary sensibility. Abandoning and abandoned, "speaking for" failure, in competition with a frenetic culture, Tate crafts a voice that is allergic to grandiosity and agreed-upon sense. He would "unmaster" the calcified traditional role of the poet as master of the word. Charles Bernstein writes in interesting ways about what the prospect of such "unmastering [of] language" entails:

> Unmastering language is not a position of inadequacy; on the contrary, mastery requires repression and is the mark of an almost unrecoverable lack. To be immersed in a language without the obsession to dominate it, conquer, take personal (even "subjective") possession of it, as if it were property: perhaps this is virtualizing space of the modernist composition. . . .[22]

Tate's art, however, subscribes only partly to Bernstein's formula, which may explain why Tate, unlike John Ashbery, a poet whom he resembles in his inventiveness, was not adopted by the language poets, for whom Bernstein has been one of the most influential spokespersons.

Tate's poetry is marked by a repetitive focusing, circling back to its subjects in almost miniaturist turns that reveal a high degree of self-conscious aesthetic control. The pathos that emerges in his work would seem inimical to many of the language poets' practices, suspicious as they are of much of lyric aesthetic tradition and intent in some instances on the destruction of the humanist personal subject. While the self may be incoherent for Tate, human longings, even a yearning for a version of transcendence, are central to his poems, and he presents vital graphs of emotions that have their echoes in lyric tradition. For all his sporting with identity, Tate allows room for subjectivity, but it is a subjectivity that is multilayered, multivoiced, and half self-canceling, as was the signature in "Tell Them   Was Here." While he affronts ready assumptions of origin, identity, and mastery, he is keenly aware of their continuing seductiveness. I would even venture that his poems are sympathetic toward desires for originary constructions of human meaning, no matter how often such constructions prove illusory for the women and men who speak in his poems. He concludes "Happy as the Day is Long" with a speaker ruminating on the meaning of what he has made and asking if his poems, once thought to be "infinite will turn out to be just a couple / of odds and ends, a tiny miscellany, miniature stuff, fragments / of novelties, of no great moment." Immediately, however, he claims the sufficiency of his poetic: "But it will also be enough, / maybe even more than enough, to suggest an immense ritual and tradition. / And this makes me very happy" (*WCF*, 82). The description, with its echo in "tiny miscellany, miniature stuff" of Joseph Cornell's uncanny assemblages, offers us the possibility that the purely "inexpert" voice—the voice that trumpets its failure at self-knowledge—discloses not only the presumptions of expertise but even the presumptions of laughter.

5

Fleshless Voices: Louise Glück's
Rituals of Abjection and Oblivion

Louise Glück's poetry travels over ancient ground in the Western tradition. Yet while her means are in some ways traditional—the adoption of the lyric voice and august themes of nature, mortality, and women's abandonment by lovers—the conceptual value of her poetry is provocative. Her speakers insinuate a wrong not allied so much to individual circumstance (circumstance seeming too easily assumed for Glück, most notably causal circumstance) as to what are posed as ineradicable laws of nature and being. Since her early career Glück has been writing a psychological autobiography, detailing the war between flesh and spirit as particularly charged because of her condition as a woman. Unlike a poet such as Marianne Moore, whom Randall Jarrell described as being preoccupied with defensive measures, Glück does not rely on a code of self-protective morals. And unlike Moore, she is, for all the mythic resonance of her work, hardly given to the fabular. Her power more surely relies on an undertone of resentment toward experiences that have found uneasy entry into literary tradition: women's violation by ordinary means, especially by copulation and pregnancy.

The violated feminine as primordial, unregulated, subject to obscure whims, the chthonic feminine that has been rehearsed in literature and philosophy: such is Glück's threatening "marshland." Her poems unite two claims that resist the inchoate "marshland" of cultural attributions affixed to womanhood: women's claim to accuse and as such to recognize injustice, and women's claim to disaffirm, to refuse gender-based expectations of harmony and affirmation. She finds the possibility of an essentialist femininity to be both repulsive and fascinating. Her poems experiment with a regression into oblivion—an ultimate release from ego boundaries—and the opposite possibility: the establishment of a powerful female self able to master narratives about origin and fate.

Glück has honed an austere voice that prohibits consolation. Consciously and repeatedly she identifies with speakers who are abandoned in crises: "From the first, I wanted to talk about death; also from the first I had an instinctive identification with the abandoned, the widowed, with all figures left behind."[1] Whereas, as we have seen, Jean Valentine counters perennial loss through the poem itself as it may comfort and illuminate—and shock by revealing the depth of her speakers' needs—and James Tate imports dizzyingly abrupt shifts in speech registers to derail traditional responses to psychic loss, in Glück almost any comforting gesture is subject to withering scrutiny. As she wrote of Sylvia Plath, a poet whom she resembles in her tense dismissals of gender pieties, Glück seeks to "repudiate the old imprisoning rituals which derive from the imposed primary association of Woman with Life."[2] She resents, then, what she sees as the cultural mandate for a female poet to celebrate life; her poetry resists such a mandate through its nearly relentless focus on psychological negations of all sorts. The response of the abandoned in this poetry is to exclude and discard, to be as much the one who abandons the other and the other's conceptions as the one who suffers personal abandonment.

Elizabeth Dodd classifies Glück's poetry as "postconfessional personal classicism—one in which the voice of the self is muted by an amplified sense of the mythic, the archetypal . . . , without losing the compelling presence of an individual, contemporary 'I,' a personal voice addressing the reader."[3] As such, the self in Glück is placed in relation to a larger mythological backdrop but is not overwhelmed by this competing narrative. The mythological narrative is used to dignify the self, particularly the female self, which might otherwise be domesticated or trivialized.

Although Glück's poetry has its roots in the confessional mode developed in the late 1950s, we might note that while confession presupposes community and the acknowledgment of a violation of the laws of the tribe, Glück relentlessly casts characters who would distinguish themselves from communal laws and biological imperatives even while they observe the seemingly inescapable impact of such laws and imperatives. Tellingly, she doesn't practice the delight in self associated with some confessionals—or even a similar self-hatred. Shame and onus are more often placed on biology and culture than on the self. She does not destroy or exorcise the other as do many confessional poets but patiently witnesses the other, presenting a situation analytically. In consequence, she occupies, as her essay "Against Sincerity"[4] makes clear, a complex position toward actuality; she would purify and crystallize or transform confessional "facts" in quest of the emotional truth, most often the bitter truth, of a situation in which a woman's abandonment, implicit or overt, figures. The voice of this abandoned woman in her poetry is, in a way that may be familiar to us from Lawrence Lipking's formulations,[5] ontologically triumphant and resistant.

The traditional dichotomy that links women with flesh and nature is particularly inimical to Glück, and over much of her career she has alluded to images of the fleshless, the nearly immaterial, as if the body itself were an encumbrance that her personae would gladly escape. As Lynn Keller points out, "Her often extremely negative sense of womanhood—as both a biologically and socially determined experience—has been crucial in shaping the language, tone, and style, as well as the thematic content of her poetry."[6] Such a stance, Keller rightly observes, unsettles readers: "Glück has not passed beyond self-loathing, and this makes reading her work still a profoundly uncomfortable experience." Keller notes that the perverse "negative" psychic tensions within Glück's poetry create much of the excitement that we experience in reading it: "This inner battle is precisely what electrifies her poetry."[7] It is revealing that, somewhat like Tate, Glück stirs critical resentment—although for quite different reasons. While Tate offends readers who may have a limited conception of "serious poetry" and an aversion to the humorous extremes that he regularly employs, Glück's critics may fault her for lacking what they find to be in excess in Tate. Throughout much of her career, her nearly relentless "seriousness" has conveyed a portentous chill, and the tones of repulsion that she registers are returned to her by some readers. Glück may dissatisfy—or infuriate—such readers because she repels ideals of affirmation and harmony in human relationships that women in her culture have been expected to uphold. As Keller suggests, however ruefully, Glück's very animosity to biology and culture lends her work power. And the disturbance that some of her readers may experience is directly related to this source of her power and seems to be inextricable from it.

For Glück, poems are inevitably a form of autobiography. In her poems, autobiography emerges not in contexts that explain rational personal choice but in the form of individual implacable voices that awaken the reader's capacity for imaginative responsiveness. More akin to Poe than Whitman, Glück proposes in her early poetry few solutions for narcissistic wounds other than the creation of a language of suspicion and rejection.

We may recall that *rejection* derives from a Latin word meaning "to throw back." In Glück's poetry we see that the rejection enacted by her early persona, her exclusion from affective ties, is "thrown back" upon others. The persona depends on rejection as a means of returning to the minim of the self that is noninclusive. She emphasizes the need to repel, refusing the cultural role of womanhood, of embrace, warmth, and kindly feeling, in order to be freed from ubiquitous others and as such to attain at least a provisional sense of separate selfhood and self-knowledge. In both her poetry and prose she suggests that knowledge is achieved by exclusion, by withstanding rather than incorporating the other.

Glück's first collection was a book of revulsions rather than illuminations. Decades after it was published she spoke of her mixed feelings about *Firstborn* (1968), describing her reaction as "embarrassed tenderness."[8] Yet that book reveals the wellsprings of her poetry. Freighted with dead matter and decay, vermin, waste, and wounds, *Firstborn* manifests its overt repulsion toward the female body and by extension toward a malignant domesticity. It is an extremist's book, ambitious in declaring distance from most manifestations of flesh and from the family as a crucible of fleshly reproduction. Unfortunately, the book's obsessive focus on physical processes lapses into bathos at points. A grandson is "Squealing in his pen";[9] "the waste's my breakfast" (*F,* 17). The family is allied to kitchen implements or cooked meats: "My sister, / stirring briefly to arrange / Her towel, browns like a chicken, under fire" (*F,* 12). Elsewhere food imagery suggests overt violence: "Today my meatman turns his trained knife / On veal, your favorite. I pay with my life" (*F,* 34).

This antipathy toward physical matter is carried over in more powerful ways in Glück's references to abortion. As Robert Miklitsch points out, Glück exhibits a "preoccupation with abortion in all its literal and metaphorical senses."[10] The abortion imagery that appears in her poems makes the fetus (as a parasite of sorts or as, remarkably, a secondary self of the speaker) yet another consumable. Her speaker is "prided flesh," caught in a parody of domestic acts, amid cutlery, a bowl. In the journey that Glück's persona takes for an abortion, she sees herself as both the one who abandons and the one who is abandoned; the woman who chooses to abort and the woman who is, in turn, deserted by any living intimate connection. The abortionist himself is involved in what seems like a domestic act of sorts, an act linking him to the traditional world of women. In "The Egg" abortion is associated with the domestic economy:

> Past cutlery I saw
> My body stretching like a tear
> Along the paper.

(F, 4)

And later:

> He's brought a bowl to catch
> The pieces of the baby.

(F, 5)

A tone of horrified fascination is set by the book's opening poem. "Chicago Train" in its entirety:

> Across from me the whole ride
> Hardly stirred: just Mister with his barren
> Skull across the arm-rest while the kid
> Got his head between his mama's legs and slept. The poison
> That replaces air took over.
> And they sat—as though paralysis preceding death
> Had nailed them there. The track bent south.
> I saw her pulsing crotch . . . the lice rooted in that baby's
>   hair.

(F, 3)

The poem seems like a parody of birth or an awkward Pietà. Notably, the parasites feeding on the child duplicate in another form the numerous feedings that will follow in the book; as we have seen, feeding to Glück suggests the violation of both physical and psychological boundaries for a self seeking a controlled sufficiency. The ellipses in the final line of "Chicago Train" form a drifting equation in which family, birth, and sensuality are linked to parasitism. Glück's reference to parasitism here and her concentration in her prose and poems on her adolescent anorexia make clear her repulsion from flesh and recall to us that the word *parasite* comes from the Greek *parasitos:* "one who eats at another's table." The derivation suggests, of course, an interloper in the family, and it is Glück's attack on the nuclear family, the self fearing its consumption or its paralysis by the family, that is the source of much of her early work.

What is perhaps especially telling in "Chicago Train" is the speaker's fascination with the physical proximity of mother and child. Glück's coded description—her spectral lingering at the scene—insinuates the speaker's subterranean envy. However limitless desires may be in these poems, the woman who speaks experiences herself as emotionally abandoned after birth. Most often in other poems her speaker is schooled in emotional depriva- tion, "at seven learning / Distance at my mother's knee" (*F,* 45). "Chicago Train" suggests, however, that physical intimacy may be as alluring—and puzzling—as emotional distance to Glück.

In her essays about her own development as a poet Glück writes re- peatedly about the habit of refusal, connecting refusal to a necessary sepa- ration from the family, given that she once saw her flesh as an extension of her mother's flesh and her mother's authority. She claims her body for her- self, desiring "ownership of [her] body, which was her [her mother's] great accomplishment."[11] Significantly, the mother in Glück's poetry and prose is cast as a body, even as an "inescapable body." Nevertheless, the mother cannot be possessed, for the daughter would resist being engulfed, and the mother herself remains psychologically elusive. Glück's poems complexly figure a psychological separation between mother and child. In "For My Mother" in *The House on Marshland* the mother is imaged as marshland, vegetal and uncomprehending, crossed between the living and the dead. The daughter who speaks in the poem envies the fetal state that she summons through her reference to the mother's womb, for this womb-state is charac- terized by elemental fusion. It is protected by an "absolute knowledge" as the child inhabits the mother, "screened / through the green glass / of your eye."[12] The poem registers the speaker's acute loss of this primary unity.

"Still Life" further complicates our sense of the mother. In this poem the mother as photographer captures and as such "frames" family dynamics:

> Father has his arm around Tereze.
> She squints. My thumb
> is in my mouth: my fifth autumn.
> Near the copper beech
> the spaniel dozes in shadows.
> Not one of us does not avert his eyes.
>
> Across the lawn, in full sun, my mother
> stands behind her camera.

(*HM,* 15)

The mother records distance between herself, her husband, and her chil- dren—and her own absence in the alignment. While the mother controls the composition, the eldest daughter, as speaker, is stalled in time and in the pose of want. Seemingly, "Still Life" is about the child's response to the mother. While the family is experienced as a "still life," simultaneously the speaker perceives her childhood as "stilled"; she cannot be wrested from a psychic paralysis that threatens to continue into adulthood.

While the mother may be seen as framing and arranging experience, the father in this poetry is more often an effaced figure of withdrawal, emotionally numbed. The daughter learns to emulate her father's withdrawal, to be "stiffened" against both affection and psychic pain, as in Daphne's story in "Mythic Fragment" in *The Triumph of Achilles*, and in the dramas of "Departure," part 1 of "Dedication to Hunger" from *Descending Figure*, and in much of *Ararat*. While the mother is a marsh, a shifting source that threatens psychologically to submerge the daughter, the synecdoche for the father is an averted face that may only be "caught" momentarily before it blurs in motion. The averted face as such ignores the daughter's existence, contributing with annihilating force to the daughter's despair.

Glück's early poetry enacts the rejection of the embryo and an embryonic, violable self, as well as the rejection of family (including the younger sister who appears briefly as an innocent or lesser self, or as future victim of violation). Glück abjects the physical body, the institution of marriage, and the comforts of nature and religious belief. Indeed, the principal action of the book is abjection of all that would threaten the insecure boundaries of this emergent self which desires an incorruptible power.

Glück's reflections on her own adolescence candidly point up this process of rejection as a means of establishing an identity:

> What I could say was *no*: the way I saw to separate myself, to establish a self with clear boundaries, was to oppose myself to the declared desire of others, utilizing their wills to give shape to my own.[13]

In her poems and prose the adolescent anorexia about which she has written figures, it would seem, in at least two ways: as a desperate measure to achieve not only separate being but to erect an idealized, powerful, clarified self—however transitory that self may be—and as a method, as she has argued, of self-education:

> Its [anorexia's] intent is to construct, in the only way possible when means are so limited, a plausible self. But the sustained act, the repudiation, designed to distinguish the self from the other also separates self and body.

. . . [A]norexia proves not the soul's superiority to but its dependence on flesh.[14]

Julia Kristeva defines abjection as it encompasses "one of those violent, dark revolts of being, directed against a threat that seems to emanate from an exorbitant outside or inside, ejected beyond the scope of the possible, the tolerable, the thinkable."[15] As such, in Kristeva's terms, Glück would seem to be a poet of abjection, for her emphasis on purifying and controlling the body of the poem in her early career is characteristic of her subject matter (inflected by her early experience) in which the physical body itself must be similarly governed. According to Kristeva, abjection is experienced as an overwhelming loathing linked to the processes of separation from the maternal: "Abjection preserves what existed in the archaism of pre-objectal relationship, in the immemorial violence with which a body becomes separated from another body in order to be—maintaining that night in which the outline of the signified thing vanishes and where only the imponderable affect is carried out."[16] Yet the source of abjection is not in itself "definable" but becomes whatever profoundly menaces an individual's sense of separate being. In Glück's early poems the lure toward abjection is nearly overwhelming, and, in this context, Kristeva's description of the way abjection overrides the psyche is especially compelling:

> Apprehensive, desire turns aside; sickened, it rejects. A certainty protects it from the shameful—a certainty of which it is proud holds on to it. But simultaneously, just the same, that impetus, that spasm, that leap is drawn toward an elsewhere as tempting as it is condemned. Unflaggingly, like an inescapable boomerang, a vortex of summons and repulsion places the one haunted by it literally beside himself.[17]

For Glück, such repulsion—from appetite, sexuality, intimacy—is also shadowed, as "Chicago Train" insinuates, by an attraction similar to that which Kristeva describes: the maternal body that Glück's persona abhors at points is experienced, at least on some level, as desirable, just as other objects of repulsion similarly fascinate. In this connection, we might note that Kristeva points to "food loathing" as "perhaps the most elementary and most archaic form of abjection" and, as we have already seen, Glück's early poetry takes many of its images from food loathing and links such loathing to the mother. But the repugnance that Kristeva explores is not only triggered by food or waste or the desired but anxiety-causing envelopment in the maternal body, but by murky ethical positions: "The shame of compromise, of being in the middle of treachery. The fascinated start that leads me toward and separates me from them."[18] The refusal to be between categories not only marks Glück's first poems in their stated rejection of maternal presence and emotional comfort, but such a refusal affects her ethical stances. Her characters are not betwixt and between; their knowledge in summations gives the tonal quality of being absolute and unshifting.

In her second book, *The House on Marshland* (1975), Glück writes a poetry that has exorcised the revulsions of *Firstborn* in favor of assuming more conscious awareness. Her speakers are not temporarily inhabited by an alien body, whether registered as fetus or lover; they have metamorphosed into analysts of the body who claim a rhetoric of knowledge. While the subtext of *Firstborn* involves a woman trapped by her ability to give birth and thus snared by a "plot / Of embryos" (*F,* 11), in her second book Glück's speakers are possessed by the "plot" of childhood. They may identify with the dead sister (referred to in her prose and poems by Glück as her actual sister who died in infancy) or with a personal history in which they cannot effectively supplant the dead but must remain stiffened against mundane life. The thematics of abortion, while superficially confined to her first book, are coded anew in her second book in terms of dramas of repudiation. The fundamental obsessive pressure remains in scenes that depict the rejection of the gendered body and the withstanding of an obscure violation.

The House on Marshland established Glück as a poet of major interest. The book is distinctive, particularly in its manipulation of tone and its inversion of many confessionalist poems' displays of extreme verbal facility and exuberant violations of social norms. Glück places her own voice under a severe restraint in the book. The poems pursue erasure, a willful minimalism, transporting the self to peripheries of experience and toward a state of ontological oblivion. Indeed, the oblivion that the poems after *Firstborn* refer to, as I shall argue later, is prompted by, and proves the counterface of, her initial impulse: abjection.

Appropriately enough for a poet so dedicated to exploring the gendered family, Glück's development as a poet was both mothered and fathered. At Columbia she studied first, for two years, with Léonie Adams and later, for four years, with Stanley Kunitz. Although her allegiance to Kunitz is most acute, she absorbed Adams's tightly compressed lyricism and symbolic density. Nonetheless, she credits Kunitz with contributing more fully than Adams to her development as a poet. Although she acknowledges that he would become a "projection" whom she wished to please ("he was one in a series of projections, beginning with my mother"),[19] from Kunitz she learned the power of recurring images and bald statement. *The House on Marshland* internalizes that early imprinting. The anecdote she tells of a turning point in her maturation as a poet is particularly revealing in this context. After completing her studies with Kunitz at Columbia, she once again brought him a group of her poems to consider. When she visited him she saw the poems laid out on a table in his apartment. She hoped, despite her own doubts about their worth, that he might find the poems commendable. Surveying the poems that she had sent him, Kunitz remarked to Glück: "'Of course, they're awful.'" And then, 'But you know that.'"[20] Despite such a negative assessment of her productions, he pronounced her a poet.

This anecdote is important not only because it divulges Glück's need to separate the mediocre from the excellent in her own poetry, but because it echoes her belief in the importance of essence beyond product; Kunitz conferred identity upon the young poet and allowed her to reject her failed poems without rejecting herself. The older poet was able to bear with her imperfections without withdrawing from her. He made it possible for her to create distance, aesthetic and psychological, between the self that made the poems and the poems as productions. In turn, his pronouncement about her early work echoes her own extreme strategies of rejection. In fact, his refusal to countenance her less distinguished efforts is crucial; he projected an ideal of accomplishment and candor that she has admired and emulated in her work and that she continues to view as powerful. It is likewise important, it seems to me, that we note that after declaring the poems "awful," Kunitz remarked "But you know that." The latter words seem almost talismanic, for the ability to know, to determine worth and outcome, is of tremendous importance to Glück's speakers, who assume much of their rhetorical weight through casting at least an illusion of self-certainty (even while the poems as a whole may be formulated to arouse readerly suspicions). That is, Glück's speakers recognize the precise value of their situations. Kunitz's words, "But you know that," allowed the young Glück the sensation of being an entirely witting participant in any judgment about her own value as a poet.

Glück's poetic coming-into-being is echoed in "All Hallows," one of the most compelling of her poems and the poem most frequently examined by critics. It opens *The House on Marshland*, inaugurating the book that revealed her distinction as a poet, notably, as the concluding stanza makes clear, her ability to create an atmosphere of foreboding:

> This is the barrenness
> Of harvest or pestilence.
> And the wife leaning out the window
> with her hand extended, as in payment,
> and the seeds
> distinct, gold, calling
> *Come here*
> *Come here, little one*
>
> And the soul creeps out of the tree.
>
> *(HM,* 3)

Surely this is a poem of immanence and growth—and of barrenness and death. As Helen Vendler points out, the poem suggests a ceremony for "bearing a child . . . but it is saturated by the poet's sense of her own birth."[21] The wife in the poem lures a soul from the vegetal world, whether the soul of the fetus or, as Vendler allows, that of the poetic self. While for Vendler "All Hallows" is a poem about the birth of self and poem and child, for Robert Miklitsch it is a poem more firmly aligned with death: "a lamentable death, a dead child."[22] Miklitsch relates the poem to the commemoration of All Hallows as the day of the dead, linking the poem to Glück's actual dead infant sister, a symbol of irrevocable loss in a number of her poems. In her turn, Diane S. Bonds, drawing upon the theories of Jacques Lacan and Nancy Chodorow, writes that the poem "dislocates both speaker and landscape, displacing them from the realm of the geographic to that of the linguistic, from the domain of the literal to that of the figurative."[23] The poem, she argues, asks "What is the cost, for the wife/mother of becoming a speaking or writing subject (that is, a "soul") as opposed to a silent object (a body)?" In such terms, the poem refers to "the cost . . . of entering the symbolic order, the androcentric system of linguistic exchange." Bonds asks whether the soul is the woman's or the child's.[24]

The permeability of reference suggested by Bond's reading (child and mother, daughter and mother, unborn and born) accounts in large measure for the poem's complex power. Within such diffuse reference boundaries the wife who must gently tempt the child/poem into being might also be seen as a midwife, connecting the poem to Glück's sense of the poet's role: "[T]o utilize the metaphor of childbirth which seems never to die: the writer is the one who attends, who facilitates: the doctor, the midwife, not the mother."[25] The iconic representation of the wife/midwife as an extended hand completes the poem—and because a hand composes the poem, unites

the wife's gesture with composition itself. But the very specificity of the
wife's pose of supplication should not be ignored. In Glück's analogy the
writer's ego is not the origin of the poem, and the poem must be paid for,
not in gold coins but in emotional expenses, by the poet/mother/midwife's
desolation and pleading. "All Hallows" emerges in the ambiguity "of harvest or pestilence," for the "payment" made by the wife cannot be prof-
fered with certainty. As such, Glück reinscribes the distance between the
writer's will and the poem; the poem cannot simply be brought into creation by consciousness. In yet another layer of associations, if we put emphasis on the soul's site (the soul "creeps out of the tree") it is as if Daphne,
one of the mythological figures that Glück is stimulated by, were to be freed
from the bark that encases her and that allowed her to repulse Apollo's
advances. (The womb and sexuality are often allied to vegetation in this
poetry, and Glück's emphasis in her sixth book on giving voice to a garden
has its beginnings in such imagery.)

After "All Hallows," the strongest poem in *The House on Marshland* casts
its own autumnal spirit in which "harvest" and "pestilence" fuse, and in
which fulfilled desire (desire for ejection of the feminine from the self) ultimately does not free or acquit. In "Gretel in Darkness" Glück turns to the
Grimms' tale of Hansel and Gretel, giving voice to Gretel years after she
has saved her brother and herself from the witch's oven. The poem in its
entirety:

> This is the world we wanted.
> All who would have seen us dead
> are dead. I hear the witch's cry
> break in the moonlight through a sheet
> of sugar: God rewards.
> Her tongue shrivels into gas. . . .
>
> Now, far from women's arms
> and memory of women, in our father's hut
> we sleep, are never hungry.
> Why do I not forget?
> My father bars the door, bars harm
> from this house, and it is years.
>
> No one remembers. Even you, my brother,
> summer afternoons you look at me as though
> you meant to leave,

as though it never happened.
But I killed for you. I see armed firs,
the spires of that gleaming kiln—

Nights I turn to you to hold me
but you are not there.
Am I alone? Spies
hiss in the stillness, Hansel,
we are there still and it is real, real,
that black forest and the fire in earnest.

(HM, 5)

This Gretel in a world of men returns to the memory of "matricide," as
Miklitsch argues, for the fairy tale's stepmother is, like the witch, another
monstrous female figure who has set out to destroy the children.[26] The witch
in the oven as the type of the destructive mother continues to inhabit the
language long after her death. The poem's unmentioned context is a hor-
rendous abandonment by a child's parent and stepparent. Darkness in this
poem is allied with the resentments of childhood, resentments framed in
response to deprivations.

   The plot of Grimms' *Hansel and Gretel* turns upon the motif of hunger. It
is hunger that drives the father and stepmother to abandon their children
and hunger that keeps the children awake in their beds long enough to
overhear their stepmother's plan to cause them to lose their way in the
forest. In the realm of the Grimms' fairy tale, all subjects and all transformations of plot and knowledge revolve around hunger and consumption.
The bread crumbs that Hansel drops to make a trail leading himself and
Gretel back to their cottage are consumed by a bird. Hansel and Gretel are
not only threatened by the fact that they may be eaten by forest beasts but
that they may be devoured by the witch, who is herself ultimately thrust
into the oven as if she were an object of consumption. Only upon the witch's
death is the threat of absolute objectification repealed, and the children
return home to their father with jewels and a companion duck (surely what
would have been, before the witch's death, a tempting game bird in a land
of famine).

   Unlike the fairy tale, Glück's poem leads to no satisfying resolution;
abandonment and psychic hunger are continuous. All threat is audible,
experienced as crying or hissing: "Spies / hiss in the stillness, Hansel / we
are there still and it is real, real, / that black forest and the fire in earnest."
The frequent sibilants (even, in this context, the sibilant in Hansel's name)

intimate the ubiquitous threat of the past as it inhabits and deforms the present. "[F]ar from women's arms / and memory of women," Gretel has at least superficially achieved her desire: to abject the threatening feminine, to abject, that is, the mother. As the rescuer of her brother, Gretel is also a "murderer" of a woman. She is a paranoid in her dark forest, locked in the trauma and incomprehension of psychological childhood. And yet, as the only female in a world of men, she is magnetized toward her culturally defined identity as a female through the persistence of memory. Her recollections thrust her into a nightmarish reliving of her ultimate act of repulsion: plunging the witch into the oven. With each image joined to the act of "witch-burning," Gretel achieves two effects: she brings the feminine into memory and she recapitulates her part in the witch's destruction. The imprinting of this killing surfaces in ever more interiorizing ways with each subsequent reference in the poem. Initially we hear the witch's cry and see her tongue "shrivel into gas." But in the second reference we are left with "the spires of that gleaming kiln"—a kiln suggesting the firing of pottery, as if Gretel, by preserving her enemy in memory, has enabled the witch to assume the status of art, and artful immortality. In the final image we complete the progression from the dissolved tongue to an exterior view of the container of the witch's destruction, and finally to the interior of the kiln— "the fire in earnest." Gretel's memory, then, leads her into the oven, as if by killing the witch she is compelled repeatedly to take the witch's place. In its evocation of memory and the indelibility of past trauma, "Gretel in Darkness" insinuates that the speaker is linked to what she has destroyed, that womanhood, which is figured as chaotic and devouring, may not be abjected from the self.

A victim of her hungers, Gretel cannot know herself. "Like most people hungry for praise and ashamed of that, of any hunger," Glück has written in an essay, "I alternated between contempt for the world that judged me and lacerating self-hatred."[27] For Glück, hunger relates metaphorically not only to physical hunger and sexual desire but to desire for knowledge, and the metaphor of hunger reinforces the bodily link that this poet makes in conceptualizing each realm.

In the second section of *The House on Marshland* her figure for the new self is the infant Moses adrift on the Nile the moment before destiny and another culture adopt him: "Extend yourself— / it is the Nile, the sun is shining, / everywhere you turn is luck" (*HM*, 27). The exiled child is here a lucky child. Yet, perhaps more significantly, the book ends with another, contemporary, male child destined to reject and to be rejected, and envisioning physical paralysis: "the dead fields, women rooted to the river" (*HM*, 42).

Descending Figure (1980), Glück's third book, graphs a progression from originary preoedipal fusion, to narcissistic projection, to a final acknowledgment of fundamental grief. The descending figure of the title is variously the drowned children of the first poem, Glück's dead infant sister, the language itself, Christ, and the persona of the poet, most fully as she experiences the temptation to enter a state of oblivion. The book quietly reverses conventions; the past is figured as being "ahead" of rather than "behind" the speaker; humans are believed to have created gods; birth is more terrifying than death. For the first time in her work, the body is repeatedly less an adversary than an object of pity. The book focuses more fully and with greater compassion on the vulnerability of children than do her previous collections. As in *The House on Marshland*, a call to a child to enter into the order of consciousness reappears, but here the fear of birth (and of trauma linked to birth and any coming-into-being) is voiced with more overt sympathy. The haunting image of the dead infant sister familiar from both earlier books is echoed in visions of ill and untended children and the pity and tenderness that they inspire. The rhythms of the poems are not insistent, as if the consciousness behind them seeks calm while in the somewhat sinister suburban emptiness all claims to authority are estranging. "So waste is elevated / into beauty" she writes in *Descending Figure*,[28] and as such she might impart the focus of her third book in which the talismans of a life are perfected. "[W]hat death claims / it does not abandon" (*DF*, 40) she writes, and this poetry indeed seems oddly death-claimed, even sepulchral at points.

In "The Drowned Children" a curiously omniscient voice emerges in an account that is only partly about its title subject:

> And yet they hear the names they used
> like lures slipping over the pond:
> *What are you waiting for*
> *come home, come home, lost*
> *in the waters, blue and permanent.*

(*DF*, 3)

The poem's ostensible theme has puzzled critics, most notably Greg Kuzma, who in a scathing attack terms the poem "a shambles"[29] and questions "how it is that Louise Glück, who herself has a son, can so glibly traffic in dead children."[30] Kuzma finds Glück's poetry "bullying," a heartless poetry symptomatic of a generalized "collapse of standards" in American poetry.[31] Surely Kuzma takes literally what is a symbolic poem: "The Drowned Children" reflects Glück's view of children's at least partially unacculturated status, and their closeness to the archaic and the presymbolic. In death the child is most obviously "unparented" and unprotected. Here the only mother who does not abandon is death itself. Yet Glück's poem is also about the self's attraction to oblivion—pointedly an adult temptation. *Oblivion*, we might recall, derives from Latin and means the "forgotten or unknown." In a lesser-known meaning it refers to "official disregard or overlooking of offenses; pardon; amnesty." In both senses the word is important to Glück, for it suggests the breakdown of defenses that her personae rigorously erect, the upkeep of which proves exhausting. To forget would be to free her personae of resentments and the concomitant need in this poetry for what seems like preemptive rejection. In the second sense of the meaning referred to above, to be oblivious would signify being granted amnesty, exemption from the bondage of memory—a state of being that is surely attractive to Glück.

Oblivion is variously framed by this poet. It is, she has written, "the lure of the regressive,"[32] a return to the womb and "the wish to be dissolved, to be allied with, absorbed into another."[33] This theme of dissolution of self is seductive—even a subject, she has said, of "grandeur" as it may be linked to the great themes of death and destruction. In a defense of Robinson Jeffers she might have been explaining her own drives in regard to oblivion as it removes the individual from an impure position: "He wanted to find something in the world which was not corrupt, not the product of corruption."[34] She writes in "The Dreamer and the Watcher":

> The drive toward oblivion seems to me (as to many others) not a symptom of sickness but a true goal, and this wish of the self to do away with the very boundaries it has struggled to discover and maintain seems to me an endless subject, however we may try to subvert its grandeur.[35]

As we have observed, there is in Glück's poems an extreme urge to contain the self and to compress and control language, to create a sealed aesthetic and conceptual container. This effort depends on the will to exclude, to extract, and to define by negation, abandoning any interfering contrary impulse. Linked to such abjection, however, is oblivion, according to Kristeva's conception:

The abject from which he [the subject] does not cease separating is for him, in short, a *land of oblivion* that is constantly remembered. Once upon blotted-out time, the abject must have been a magnetized pole of covetousness. But the ashes of oblivion now serve as a screen and reflect aversion, repugnance. The clean and proper (in the sense of incorporated and incorporable) becomes filthy, the sought-after turns into the banished, fascination into shame.[36]

In Glück, the urge to reject, to draw up walls around being, to create an unassailable self with its firm sense of personal history, is met by a contrary pressure: to regress, to be swallowed entirely into another so as to enter into a state of oblivion and liquefy the boundaries of identity. To abject is to repel, to be unabsorbed by the other, while oblivion suggests its reverse: to unite absolutely. Both abjection and oblivion project forms of perfection that allow for no in-between states of being. Glück is tempted toward one or both states alternately, but she is gifted with powers of self-analysis that allow her to explore such twin pressures, marking her poems with the deep imprint of her dilemma.

Where these two pressures meet, however, is in their outcome, as Glück conceptualizes it: both, paradoxically, lead to isolation. Oblivion, in what she calls its "various forms . . . of dream to orgasm to death," amounts to experiences that, while they are sometimes described in terms of union, are felt as more fully isolating moments. "[T]he oblivion we ultimately achieve is an outpost of solitude from which the other is exiled—your oblivion is not mine, as your dream is not,"[37] she has argued in an essay. That is, even oblivion does not allow for a final experience of union between individuals but for a further declaration of one's aloneness. References to snow, whirling rain, or flying leaves, agitations in the air and disturbances in the visual field, tend to accompany her focus on oblivion as if to reinforce the isolating intensity of inner weather that her personae experience.

Despite her emphasis on control, particularly control of body and reproduction, repeatedly Glück writes of the need to renounce will, for she believes that no measure of will can allow the poet to compose an authentic poem. Referring to poetic insight, she maintains that "it comes slyly, or with an air of being unwilled, the air of query or postulate or vision." In consequence, any aesthetic teleology should be defeated: "Poetic intelligence lacks, I think, such focused investment in conclusion, being naturally wary of its own assumptions. It derives its energy from a willingness to discard conclusion in the face of evidence, its willingness, in fact, to discard anything."[38] Glück's prose is dominated by the theme of the will's failure to create poems and the poet's necessary discipline: the discipline of abandoning preconceptions. "The fundamental experience of the writer is helplessness," she begins her essay "The Education of the Poet." Indeed, the poem cannot be forced into being but requires of the poet a practiced receptivity: "In a whole lifetime, years are spent waiting to be claimed by an idea. The only real exercise of will is negative: we have toward what we write the power of veto."[39] Unlike what Glück sees as an authentic poem (the poem of exploration), the willed poem foresees its own strategies and is thus inevitably a counterfeit because it denies the poet the necessary turbulence of discovery. She is dismissive of contemporaries who seem to her to be "willing" their poems into being as if they were smugly controlling all responses to their poems and in consequence rendering their personae blameless in events that are represented in their poems. In a review she criticizes one contemporary poet's "managerial interventions, her insistence on a single rigid interpretation; limited in a sense by excess will."[40] The poet "yearns"— a familiar word in Glück's prose—but the poet cannot control the path of illumination. She has declared repeatedly that she distrusts prolific writing, and most of her essays are informed explicitly by her struggle with silences. Enduring periods of creative sterility is, she argues, a form of near heroism: "For poets, speech and fluency seem less an act of courage than a state of grace. The intervals of silence, however, require a stoicism very like courage; of these, no reader is aware."[41]

In spite of her reiterations of the unwilled quality of mature poetry, the iconic character of Glück's prose and the vatic voice of her poetry are at odds with her argument. In "Disruption, Hesitation, Silence," she writes: "It seems to me that what is wanted, in art, is to harness the power of the unfinished."[42] The infinitive itself is telling: *to harness* implies will, that is, the power consciously and with premeditation to rewrite one's story. Her axiomatic prose, built plaint by plaint, reveals in turn the most willful care. The irony of her rejection of will is that Glück's prose and poetry generate much of their impact from what seems like the most strategic rhetoric. She seldom qualifies statements even when discussing doubt itself. For their impact, her poems rely on tone, and her own tone is one—for all her emphasis on the promise uncertainty holds—of extreme knowledge, even of fatedness. In fact, the omission of context in her poems raises multiple questions in the reader, and yet seldom allows for an impression that the speakers of her poems share in this bafflement about either cause or effect. Glück's very attraction, after *Firstborn*, to the "eternally recurring" situation[43] reveals her preference for projecting mythic infallibility. The combined impact of her images and statements in poems make for speakers who know all too well the order of things. As she has noted, she often writes "backwards," moving from revelation to origins, from result to some intimation of causal circumstance: "My own work begins at the . . . end, literally, at illumination, which has then to be traced back to some source in the world. This method, when it succeeds, makes a thing that seems irrefutable. Its failure is felt as portentousness."[44]

Although her speakers do not often appear to doubt themselves, Glück would make us doubt the speakers' convictions—and therein, perhaps, her repeated emphasis on the poet's "helplessness," the poet's inability to assume mastery of her poetry, may seem more congruent with her stated practices. In her poems, many of them resembling miniature revenge dramas or bills of retribution, she allows us to believe in her speakers' emotions but not necessarily in their ultimate claims to truth, as a poem like "The Untrustworthy Speaker" explicitly projects: "When I speak passionately, / that's when I'm least to be trusted."[45] In its most extreme form in *Ararat*, each poem's "ego" has been replaced by a psychiatric function, the account already dwelled upon, as if rendered into summative statements from the clinician's couch, and yet, like many statements rendered in psychoanalysis, inherently suspect. As she writes in "The Triumph of Achilles": "the legends / cannot be trusted— / their source is the survivor, / the one who has been abandoned."[46] Speaking for the abandoned, she has developed voices that are explicitly partial and idiosyncratic, their grief troubling the surfaces of the poems.

Glück's book that most fully reflects her desire to learn to relinquish her own will—a fierce-enough force—is *The Triumph of Achilles* (1985). The book represents a breaking point from her earlier poetic, an attempt to come to terms with physical and psychological imperfections and with the limited products of earth. That is, through human affection her personae become "mortal," and the self-consciousness of including more questions in the poems' lines—a technique that Glück points out that she had resisted in other collections and consciously assigned herself in *The Triumph of Achilles*—allows for a complex tone of psychological vulnerability. For all the sensuality of *The Triumph of Achilles* (Achilles' triumph is his ability to love, which marks him as mortal), the book simultaneously records its ambivalence toward the sensual world. The poems deal with a successful love affair that moves beyond projection to acknowledge limited selfhood, the imperfect human rather than paralyzing perfection. As she had noted in *Descending Figure*, the body is inevitably a source of pain, but it is worse to be incorruptible, unchangeable, like the stone animals that she views in a garden: "Admit that it is terrible to be like them, / beyond harm" (*DF*, 5).

The book opens with the startling "Mock Orange" in which the speaker remarks bitterly of the flowers: "I hate them as I hate sex." As if the sensual world were a source of coercion, the body is seen as a faithless collaborator. Posing herself against the body's demands, Glück's speaker is resentful even toward instinctual life:

> I hate them.
> I hate them as I hate sex,
> the man's mouth
> sealing my mouth, the man's
> paralyzing body—
>
> and the cry that always escapes, . . .
>
> (*TA*, 3)

Eavan Boland remarks with special insight on the cry that erupts in "Mock Orange":

> It can also be heard as the cry of the erotic object itself—that silenced, paralyzed, gagged object—finding air and expression and dissent. Voicing its pain after its age-long role as servant of desire and trophy of the power of poetry. The narrator of this poem does not flinch from the volatile mix of the sexual and erotic, but once again, they are radically disassembled. The erotic object is now the speaker. The sexualizing perspective is now the substance of the rebuke. The powers of nature so often celebrated and invoked in the traditional love poem are accused and reproached.[47]

Sensuality and sexuality here lead to objectification of the body. For Glück's speaker, one is made a thing through sexuality. The poem thus opens with an absolutive statement countered by the mixed feelings that later emerge when the speaker refuses to enter into "the tired antagonisms" between women and men. Abjection, as we have noted, is a way to refuse to be an object, but instead to be propulsive, to act on an environment, to separate and define one's being against others, and to establish essential differences.

For Glück, the body with its reflexes is a "proof" of love, but sexuality creates silence. She would resent the false assurance of union gained from sexual feeling, for her perception of the very depth of her isolation and her attraction to states of abjection allow her to assume voice. "Mock Orange" insists on projecting mixed feelings. Flesh stifles and mutes; fleshly congress implies a horrific loss of control—yet a loss that is both feared and desired, for it is a movement beyond language into the seductive unknown of oblivion.

In *Ararat* (1990), published five years after *The Triumph of Achilles*, Glück is aware of her persona as mired in former perceptions, viewing her speaker as "a device that listened. / Not inert: still" (*A*, 15). The collection is a record of self-stasis. It asserts its summations immediately, processing the meaning of events in a manner sometimes vaguely familiar from popular psychoanalytic theory. Some of the same astringent tones arise as in earlier collections, but this is, in a sense, expository poetry, self-conscious in its insights. The book largely depends on a psychoanalytical focus: "I know myself; I've learned to hear like a psychiatrist" (*A*, 34). In "Confession" she allies herself with the Fates, identified with envy, an emotion for which her speaker excoriates herself. At the same time, as in "Lullaby," the poems recapitulate the pull toward formlessness and oblivion that we have detected in much of her work: "The soul's like all matter: / why should it stay intact, stay faithful to its own form, / when it could be free?" (*A*, 29).

Glück lays claim to the provinces of prose fiction, telling a linked story of characters who are buoyant and fluent and others who are leaden and silent. While she interlocks the poems' subjects to mirror the propulsion of narrative, even titling one poem "A Novel," she also points in the same poem to the intractability of her material as a source for fictional development: "No one could write a novel about this family: / too many similar characters. Besides, they're all women; / there was only one hero" (*A*, 18). Evidence of abandonment and neglect is borne out through the collection in her reflections on her father's death and on the psychological stance that the mother assumes after the father's funeral. "[T]he wish to move backward," the mother's wish in "A Fantasy" (*A*, 16), is the wish of many of her personae who seek oblivion.

Appearing two years after *Ararat*, *The Wild Iris* (1992) makes the subject of discovering poetic voice explicit. The previous collection emphasizes the stubborn power of silence as a means of withholding love and displaying the speaker's watchfulness, for a good listener can detect weaknesses and exploit the voluble. In the midst of lovelessness, of emotional scarcity, the silent, by not voicing their needs, claim for themselves an alembic dignity. In contrast, *The Wild Iris* allows for many voices to emerge from a garden, and the distancing effect of placing most utterances in nonhuman elements has freed Glück to write openly of vulnerability and need. By turning to a convention in *The Wild Iris*, the voicing of flowers, she set for herself the challenge of resisting in her readers a predictable nostalgia. Yet her strategy allows her to defy matter, escaping the human body to imagine speaking but "fleshless" bodies. Her rapid composition of the poems in ten weeks during the summer of 1991 suggests that her approach fulfilled psychic needs, as if she had long yearned to write as a disembodied voice, freed of fleshly confines.

It is the voiced quality, the imagined act of being born as a hesitant and searching voice, that is at the center of most poems in *The Wild Iris*—as the red poppy, for one clear instance, explains: "I speak / because I am shattered."[48] Indeed, the cyclic dormancy that is viewed as part of the plants' cycle may be seen as part of Glück's own writing cycle. The "fate" of the plants is not in question; we are familiar with their cycles of generation. Similarly, Glück views an authentic writing life as one that is marked by unavoidable periods of silence. We bring to these poems echoes from Glück's previous books with their eschatologies and aftermaths; that is, we import to the poems our knowledge of an order of irrevocable fate by which her characters have always been constrained.

The Wild Iris opens at the point at which oblivion has been cast off in favor of speech:

> . . . whatever
> returns from oblivion returns
> to find a voice: . . .
>
> (*WI*, 1)

Glück writes of the exhilaration of speaking as if she were a redeemed Daphne: "in a sense passionately / attached to the living tree, my body / actually curled in the split trunk" (*WI*, 2). God or the godlike in *The Wild Iris* is addressed as one who may choose other objects of desire, other creations, and, as such, God is an echo of an early crisis for her persona: the crisis of the child who believes herself abandoned by an emotionally withdrawn father, who believes herself to be neglected and inadequate, the less favored not only after a living younger sister but also after—most undefeatable of rivals—a firstborn dead infant sister.

Meadowlands, which appeared four years after *The Wild Iris*, focuses on the abandonment of a contemporary woman who shades into the figure of Penelope. (In Glück's reworking of the myth, Odysseus will ultimately leave Penelope rather than be united with her.) *The Odyssey* sustains Glück's own intermittent progression in narrative, while abrupt changes in the emotional temperature of the book are accomplished in part through references to the effluvia of daily life.

Clearly, as has been the case throughout her career, the abandoned hold Glück's true interest. Assuming the voice of a contemporary Penelope in *Meadowlands*, Glück's persona is the prototype of the deserted wife. Throughout the collection, Penelope is engaged in ritualistic ways of being that defend her against the anxiety caused by her husband's departure. Her stalwart acts of attention place her in a position that is familiar to us from other representative women in Glück's poetry: she is not diminished by misfortune, although her suffering registers in moments of hapless melancholy. Rather, she clings to art as self-preservation. Glück's Penelope is a maker, and her loom is a type of poem, a locus of creation and de-creation. It is Odysseus who is constricted by role more severely than Penelope. Through primarily female eyes (Circe and a Siren speak, as well as Penelope) his complaints emerge as carping; his passions, even when defended, come across at some level as witless.

The natural world in *The Wild Iris* gives utterance to longing and to bafflement at the forces of destruction and rebirth. Nature reflects its light on lovers. But the title of Glück's seventh book refers to flatlands (and, as she points out, humorously, baseball fields), and it is the strange "flat" peace of Penelope in nature that is emblematic of her sustained personhood. We could think of her as in the position of the poet who expresses patience before the retreating poem, as if her husband, forever in retreat, were a form of muse. Indeed, Odysseus may seem to be "the unfolding dream or image / shaped by the woman working the loom, / sitting there in a hall filled / with literal-minded men."[49] Yet the actual character of the husband/Odysseus in *Meadowlands*, vacillating as he may be in a traditional muselike manner, does not fulfill Glück's vision of inspiration. After all, it is Penelope's own voice that pursues Odysseus, demanding recognition in a muselike manner. If we return to Glück's "Gretel in Darkness" for a moment, we may be able to hear its echoes in "Quiet Evening," from *Meadowlands*:

So Penelope took the hand of Odysseus,
not to hold him back but to impress
this peace on his memory:

from this point on, the silence through which you move
is my voice pursuing you.

(*M*, 5)

The speaker of "Gretel in Darkness," we may recall, is threatened audibly
by her own memory, as if memory were in hostile pursuit of her sanity. In
"Quiet Evening" the wife, like Gretel, is located in a forest, but she threatens to make her own voice haunt her husband. She will be the one to make
her presence known, as subject rather than as object.

     Glück's body of work bespeaks remarkable will and control. Indeed,
the common phrase *body of work* may be particularly appropriate in Glück's
case, for she has lived with her work as if it were her body, a body that she
could only partially control. The origins of the body and the poem as a
kind of secondary body are in marshland, in the oblivion of formlessness
and inchoate womblike elements that are culturally aligned to women and
that Glück finds to be so deeply embedded in the language that she is hard-
pressed to disengage herself from them. It is especially significant that she
describes her relationship to writing in terms of difficulty. As we noticed
earlier, the theme of abandonment by an obscure force that makes resonant poetry possible is common in her essays and an undercurrent in her
poems in which speech is imperiled by silence. Perhaps the tension that we
detect in her speakers derives in part from the threat of speechlessness; we
sense that any voice in her poems emerges under embattled psychic circumstances.
     Glück has attempted in each of her books to change the style of her
work and to change the self—already so perilously impermanent—that
makes the poems. She has treated her books as if they were skins that she
might shed, as if they, like the body that she sought to master in adolescence, might be perfected. Each book begins, Glück has written, with "a
conscious diagnostic act, a swearing off" of her earlier aesthetic strategies.[50]
Just the same, Glück's voice has been recognizable in each of her books;
each is imprinted with her signature concerns and her signature stylistic
austerity. (Even *Meadowlands*, with its inclusion of humor and seemingly
trivial daily details, allows for such material in only rather small amounts,

surely not enough to dilute the tonal voiceprint that we recognize as Glück's own.) What the sequence of books makes clear is this poet's progressive strategies. First she would describe and then render substantial the wavering self as a still life, perfected into paralysis. Later she enacts a complex resistance to the very state of paralyzed being that she had earlier recorded. The "triumph of Achilles"—or of Louise Glück—rests on a renewed assumption of mortal, fleshly fallibility. She makes her own aesthetic position, tenuous as it may be, out of the materials that she associates with abandonment—the representation of desertion by others and the representation of a corollary desire to abandon cultural prohibitions—and out of a dignity in finding speech for the conflicted psyche and its most stubborn hungers.

Notes

INTRODUCTION

1. Lawrence Lipking, *Abandoned Women and Poetic Tradition* (Chicago: University of Chicago Press, 1988), p. xvii.

2. Mary K. DeShazer, *Inspiring Women: Reimagining the Muse* (New York: Pergamon, 1986), p. ix.

3. Russell Edson, "Portrait of the Writer as a Fat Man: Some Subjective Ideas or Notions on the Care and Feeding of Prose Poems," in *Claims for Poetry*, ed. Donald Hall (Ann Arbor: University of Michigan Press, 1982), p. 100.

4. Stan Sanvel Rubin, "Introduction: Beyond the War Zone," in *The Post-Confessionals: Conversations with American Poets of the Eighties*, ed. Earl G. Ingersoll, Judith Kitchen, Stan Sanvel Rubin (Rutherford, N.J.: Fairleigh Dickinson University Press, 1989), p. 21.

5. Ibid., p. 17.

6. Ibid., p. 18.

7. Stuart Friebert and David Young, eds., *Models of the Universe: An Anthology of the Prose Poem* (Oberlin, Ohio: Oberlin College Press, 1995), p. 306.

8. Lipking, *Abandoned Women*, p. 187.

9. Charles Wright, "A. P. & E. D.," *Missouri Review* 10, no. 3 (1987): 167.

10. Jean Valentine, "An Interview by Michael Klein," *American Poetry Review* 20, no. 4 (1991): 43.

11. Louise Glück, "Invitation and Exclusion," in *Proofs & Theories: Essays on Poetry* (Hopewell, N.J.: Ecco, 1994), p. 121.

12. Henry Hart, "Story-Tellers, Myth-Makers, Truth-Sayers," *New England Review* 15, no. 4 (1993): 192.

13. Harold Bloom, *Figures of Capable Imagination* (New York: Seabury, 1976), p. xi.

14. One of the most illuminating recent studies on the problematics of tradition and canon for American poets is Stephen Fredman's *The Grounding of American Poetry: Charles Olson and the Emersonian Tradition* (Cambridge: Cambridge University Press, 1993).

15. Dennis Brown, *The Modernist Self in Twentieth-Century English Literature: A Study in Self-Fragmentation* (New York: St. Martin's Press, 1989), p. 6.

16. Robert Phillips, *The Confessional Poets* (Carbondale: Southern Illinois University Press, 1973), p. 1.

17. Ibid., p. 8.

18. James McCorkle, *The Still Performance: Writing, Self, and Interconnection in Five Postmodern American Poets* (Charlottesville: University Press of Virginia, 1989), p. 2.

19. Ibid., p. 5.

20. Phillips, *Confessional Poets*, p. 2.

21. Edson, "Portrait of the Writer as a Fat Man," p. 99.

22. Paul Breslin, *The Psycho-Political Muse: American Poetry Since the Fifties* (Chicago: University of Chicago Press, 1987), p. 121.

23. Charles Wright, "An Interview with Charles Wright," interview by Sherod Santos, *Missouri Review* 10, no. 1 (1987): 85.

24. Edson, "Portrait of the Artist as a Fat Man," p. 100.

25. Vernon Shetley, *After the Death of Poetry: Poet and Audience in Contemporary America* (Durham, N.C.: Duke University Press, 1993), p. 192.

26. Greg Kuzma, "Rock Bottom: Louise Glück and the Poetry of Dispassion," *Midwest Quarterly* 24, no. 4 (1983): 474.

27. See Alan Williamson's use of the term *anti-epiphany* in *Introspection and Contemporary Poetry* (Cambridge: Harvard University Press, 1984), p. 96.

CHAPTER 1. THE DOUBTING PENITENT: CHARLES WRIGHT'S EPIPHANIES OF ABANDONMENT

1. Charles Wright, "Bytes and Pieces," in *Quarter Notes: Improvisations and Interviews* (Ann Arbor: University of Michigan Press, 1995), p. 80.

2. Ibid., p. 81.

3. See ibid, pp. 81–82, in which the poet writes: "[M]y subject (language, landscape, and the idea of God) is not of much interest now. But it will be again. How all three configure one's own face is important and must be addressed."

4. Maurice Blanchot, "From Dread to Language," in *The Gaze of Orpheus and Other Literary Essays*, trans. Lydia Davis, ed. P. Adams Sitney (Barrytown, N.Y.: Station Hill, 1981), p. 18.

5. Maurice Blanchot, "The Essential Solitude," in *Gaze of Orpheus*, p. 67.

6. Charles Wright, "Charles Wright at Oberlin," *Field* 17 (fall 1997): 65.

7. Charles Wright, "The Art of Poetry XLI: Charles Wright," interview by J. D. McClatchy, *Paris Review* 113 (1989): 195.

8. Charles Wright, "Improvisations on Form and Measure," *Ohio Review* 38 (1987): 23.

9. Charles Wright, "An Interview," interview by Elizabeth McBride, *Ohio Review* 34 (1985): 17.

10. Calvin Bedient, "Tracing Charles Wright," *Parnassus: Poetry in Review* 10, no. 1 (1982): 55.

11. David St. John, foreword to *Country Music: Selected Early Poems*, by Charles Wright, 2d ed. (Hanover, N.H.: Wesleyan University Press, 1991), p. xiii.

12. William James, *The Varieties of Religious Experience: A Study in Human Nature* (New York: Collier), 1961), p. 220.

13. Ibid., p. 221.

14. Ibid., p. 225.

15. Ibid., p. 233.

16. Bedient, "Tracing Charles Wright," p. 55.

17. Charles Wright, "Invisible Landscape," in *Country Music: Selected Early Poems*, 2d ed.

(Hanover, N.H.: Wesleyan University Press, 1991), p. 134. Hereafter the title of this collection will be abbreviated as *CM*, and page numbers will be cited parenthetically in the text.

18. Charles Wright, "Local Journal," in *The World of Ten Thousand Things: Poems, 1980–1990* (New York: Farrar, Straus & Giroux, 1990), p. 229. Hereafter the title of this collection will be abbreviated as *WTT*, and page numbers will be cited parenthetically in the text.

19. Charles Altieri, *Self and Sensibility in Contemporary American Poetry* (Cambridge: Cambridge University Press, 1984), p. 49.

20. Charles Wright, "Halflife: A Commonplace Notebook," *Field* 36 (1987): 21.

21. Richard Tillinghast, "From 'An Elegist's New England, a Buddhist's Dante,'" in *The Point Where All Things Meet: Essays on Charles Wright*, ed. Tom Andrews (Oberlin, Ohio: Oberlin College Press, 1995), p. 197.

22. Charles Wright, "Improvisations on Pound," in *Halflife: Improvisations and Interviews, 1977–87* (Ann Arbor: University of Michigan Press, 1988), p. 15.

23. Charles Wright, "Georgio Morandi," in *Halflife*, p. 7.

24. Charles Wright, "Notes," in *The Other Side of the River* (New York: Random House, 1984). Wright underwent this procedure in 1981, according to his *Quarter Notes*, p. 13.

25. Maurice Blanchot, "The Gaze of Orpheus," in *Gaze of Orpheus*, p. 100.

26. Maurice Blanchot, "Two Versions of the Imaginary," in *Gaze of Orpheus*, p. 79.

27. Helen Vendler, "Charles Wright: The Transcendent 'I.'" *Part of Nature, Part of Us: Modern American Poets* (Cambridge: Harvard University Press, 1980), p. 277.

28. Wright, "An Interview with Charles Wright" (Santos), p. 75.

29. Charles Wright, "Metaphysics of the Quotidian: A Conversation with Charles Wright," in Ingersoll, Kitchen, and Rubin, eds., *Post-Confessionals*, p. 35.

30. Wright, "Improvisations on Pound," p. 19.

31. Ibid., p. 15.

32. Wright, "Halflife: A Commonplace Notebook," p. 28.

33. See Wright's comments about the influence of Emily Dickinson and Walt Whitman on his work: "Improvisations on Form and Measure," p. 21.

34. Wright, "Improvisations on Pound," p. 15.

35. Wright, "An Interview with Charles Wright" (Santos), p. 90.

36. McCorkle, *Still Performance*, p. 172.

37. Bruce Bond, "Metaphysics of the Image in Charles Wright and Paul Cézanne," *Southern Review* 30, no. 2 (1994): 121.

38. St. John, preface to *Country Music*, p. xviii.

39. Bedient, "Tracing Charles Wright," p. 55.

40. Ibid., p. 58.

41. Charles Wright, quoted in Joseph Parisi, "Charles Wright," in *Poets in Person: A Listener's Guide* (Chicago: Modern Poetry Association, 1992), p. 149.

42. Ibid., p. 151.

43. Charles Wright, "Bytes and Pieces," in *Quarter Notes*, p. 83.

44. Charles Wright, preface to *Country Music*, p. xxiii.

45. Charles Wright, "The Art of Poetry XLI," p. 205.

46. Charles Wright, "An Interview" (McBride), p. 129.

47. Northrop Frye, *Anatomy of Criticism: Four Essays* (Princeton: Princeton University Press, 1957), p. 271.

48. Wright, "An Interview with Charles Wright" (Santos), p. 85.

49. X. J. Kennedy, "A Tenth and Four Fifths," review of *The Southern Cross*, by Charles Wright, *Poetry* 141 (1983): 358.

50. Vendler, *Part of Nature, Part of Us*, p. 288.

51. Norman Finkelstein, *The Utopian Moment in Contemporary American Poetry* (Lewisburg, Pa.: Bucknell University Press, 1988), p. 47.

52. Julia Kristeva, *Black Sun: Depression and Melancholia*, trans. Leon S. Roudiez (New York: Columbia University Press, 1989), p. 6.

53. Calvin Bedient, "Sliding-Wheeling Around the Curves," in Andrews, ed., *Point Where All Things Meet*, p. 39.

54. Ibid., p. 68.

55. Robert Pinsky, *The Situation of Poetry: Contemporary Poetry and its Traditions* (Princeton: Princeton University Press, 1976), p. 112.

56. Charles Wright, "Sitting Outside at the End of Autumn," in *Chickamauga* (New York: Farrar, Straus & Giroux, 1995), p. 3. Hereafter the title of this collection will be abbreviated as *C*, and page numbers will be cited parenthetically in the text.

57. Charles Wright, "Lives of the Saints," in *Black Zodiac* (New York: Farrar, Straus & Giroux, 1997), p. 42.

58. Ibid., p. 45.

59. Ibid., p. 42.

60. Ibid., p. 43.

CHAPTER 2. CRUEL FIGURES: THE "ANTI-FORMS" OF RUSSELL EDSON

1. Donald Hardy, "Russell Edson's Humor: Absurdity in a Surreal World," *Studies in American Humor* 6 (1988): 96.

2. André Breton, "On Surrealism in its Living Works (1953)," *Manifestoes of Surrealism*, trans. Richard Seaver and Helen R. Lane (Ann Arbor: University of Michigan Press, 1969), p. 303.

3. Denise Levertov, introduction to *The Very Thing That Happens: Fables and Drawings*, by Russell Edson (Norfolk, Conn: New Directions, 1964), p. vi.

4. T. W. Adorno, *Aesthetic Theory*, trans. C. Lenhardt, ed. Gretel Adorno and Rolf Tiedemann (London: Routledge and Kegan Paul, 1984), p. 27.

5. Sven Birkerts, "Prose Poetry," *Parnassus: Poetry in Review* 15, no. 1 (1989): 179.

6. Levertov, introduction, p. vi.

7. Donald Hall, "On Russell Edson's Genius," *American Poetry Review* 6, no. 5 (1979): 12.

8. Mary Ann Caws. "The Self-Defining Prose Poem: On Its Edge," in *The Prose Poem in France: Theory and Practice*, ed. Mary Ann Caws and Hermine Riffaterre (New York: Columbia University Press, 1983), p. 181.

9. Ibid., p. 180.

10. Russell Edson, "The Prose Poem in America," *Parnassus: Poetry in Review* 5 (1976): 322.

11. Ibid., p. 321.

12. Edson, "Portrait of the Writer as a Fat Man," p. 103.

13. Ibid., p. 101.

14. Edson, "The Prose Poem in America," p. 321.

15. Jean-François Lyotard, *The Postmodern Condition: A Report on Knowledge*, trans. Geoff Bennington and Brian Massumi (Minneapolis: University of Minnesota Press, 1984), p. 81.

16. Edson, "Portrait of the Writer as a Fat Man," p. 99.

17. For a discussion of similar effects in literature see Terry Eagleton, *Marxism and Literary Criticism* (Berkeley: University of California Press, 1976), pp. 26–27.

18. Michael Benedikt, introduction to *The Prose Poem: An International Anthology,* ed. Michael Benedict (New York: Dell, 1976), p. 39.

19. Ibid., p. 40.

20. Ibid., p. 48.

21. Jonathan Monroe, *A Poverty of Objects: The Prose Poem and the Politics of Genre* (Ithaca: Cornell University Press, 1987), p. 280.

22. Edson, "Portrait of the Writer as a Fat Man," p. 103.

23. Russell Edson, "Poem of Intention," in *Intuitive Journey and Other Works* (New York: Harper, 1976), p. 90. Hereafter the title of this collection will be abbreviated as *IJ*, and page numbers will be cited parenthetically in the text.

24. Susan E. Hawkins, "Russell Edson's Fabled World," *American Poetry* 5, no. 3 (1988): 39. See also Hardy, "Russell Edson's Humor," pp. 93–103.

25. Hardy, "Russell Edson's Humor," p. 99.

26. Susan Stewart, *Nonsense: Aspects of Intertextuality in Folklore and Literature* (Baltimore: Johns Hopkins University Press, 1979), p. 89.

27. See Charles Simic's comments in the *Atlanta Review* 2, no. 1 (1995): 26: "Jim Tate, Strand, everybody I knew back then was reading that book. It was a book that confirmed what you already intuited."

28. Gaston Bachelard, *The Poetics of Space,* trans. Maria Jolas (New York: Orion, 1964), p. 3.

29. Ibid., p. 4.

30. Russell Edson, "The Ceremony," in *The Reason Why the Closet-Man is Never Sad* (Middletown, Conn.: Wesleyan University Press, 1977), p. 15. Hereafter the title of this collection will be abbreviated as *RWC,* and page numbers will be cited parenthetically in the text.

31. Russell Edson, "Doctor House," in *A Stone is Nobody's* (Stanford, Conn.: privately published, 1961), p. 13.

32. Bin Ramke, "A Gesture of Permission: On Poems in Prose, Etc.," *Denver Quarterly* 25, no. 4 (1991): 131.

33. Russell Edson, "The Unforgiven," in *The Wounded Breakfast* (Middletown, Conn.: Wesleyan University Press, 1985), p. 16.

34. Hawkins, "Russell Edson's Fabled World," p. 41.

35. Russell Edson, "The House of Sara Loo," *Parnassus: Poetry in Review* 16, no. 1 (1990): 97.

36. Barbara Johnson, "Disfiguring Poetic Landscape," in *Prose Poem in France,* p. 96.

37. Roland Barthes, *Mythologies,* trans. Annette Lavers (New York: Farrar, Straus & Giroux, 1972), p. 155.

38. Russell Edson, "Vomit," in *The Clam Theater* (Middletown, Conn.: Wesleyan University Press, 1973), p. 77.

39. Russell Edson, "The Broken Daughter," in *Clam Theater,* p. 21.

40. Edson, "Portrait of the Writer as a Fat Man," p. 97.

41. Russell Edson, "One Man's Story," *Prose Poem: An International Journal* 1 (1992): 29.

42. Russell Edson, "Counting Sheep." in *Fifty Contemporary Poets: The Creative Process,* ed. Alberta T. Turner (New York: McKay, 1977), p. 93.

43. Russell Edson, quoted in Duane Ackerman, "Russell Edson," in *Contemporary Poets,* ed. James Vinson, 3d ed. (New York: St. Martin's Press, 1980), p. 427.

44. *Contemporary Authors*, ed. Ann Evory (Detroit: Gale, 1978),s.v. "Edson, Russell."

45. Hardy, "Russell Edson's Humor," p. 97.

46. Stewart, *Nonsense*, p. 121.

47. Edson, "Portrait of the Writer as a Fat Man," p. 101.

48. Ibid., p. 103.

49. Ibid., p. 98.

50. Russell Edson, "The Tunnel," in *Wounded Breakfast*, p. 166.

51. Edson, "Portrait of the Writer as a Fat Man, p. 100.

52. Ibid., p. 98.

CHAPTER 3. "DREAM BARKER": PREOEDIPAL FUSION AND RADIANT BOUNDARIES IN JEAN VALENTINE

1. Valentine, "Jean Valentine: An Interview by Michael Klein," intro., 39 n. 10.

2. Jean Valentine, "The Hallowing of the Everyday," in *Acts of Mind: Conversations with Contemporary Poets*, ed. Richard Jackson (Tuscaloosa: University of Alabama Press, 1983), p. 31.

3. Dudley Fitts, foreword to *Dream Barker*, by Jean Valentine (New Haven: Yale University Press, 1965), p. vii.

4. Valentine, "The Hallowing of the Everyday," p. 29.

5. Philip Booth, "On Jean Valentine: A Continuum of Turning," *American Poetry Review* 9, no. 1 (1980): 4.

6. Steven Cramer, "Self-Defense," *Poetry* 161, no. 3 (1992): 161.

7. Valentine, "The Hallowing of the Everyday," p. 29.

8. Helen Vendler, *The Breaking of Style: Hopkins, Heaney, Graham* (Cambridge: Harvard University Press, 1995), p. 1.

9. Jean Valentine, *Dream Barker* (New Haven: Yale University Press, 1965), p. 46. Hereafter the title of this collection will be abbreviated as *DB*, and page numbers will be cited parenthetically in the text.

10. Julia Kristeva, *Black Sun: Depression and Melancholia*, trans. Leon S. Roudiez (New York: Columbia University Press, 1989), pp. 60–61.

11. Julia Kristeva, *Desire in Language: A Semiotic Approach to Literature and Art*, ed. Leon S. Roudiez, trans. Thomas Gora, Alice Jardine, and Leon S. Roudiez (New York: Columbia University Press, 1980), p. 134.

12. Ibid., 137.

13. Jean Valentine, "The Couples," in *Pilgrims* (New York: Farrar, Straus & Giroux, 1969), p. 3. Hereafter the title of this collection will be abbreviated as *P*, and page numbers will be cited parenthetically in the text.

14. Jean Valentine, "Huub Oosterhuis: Orpheus," in *The Messenger* (New York: Farrar, Straus & Giroux, 1979), p. 36. Hereafter this collection is abbreviated as *M*, and references to page numbers are made parenthetically.

15. Valentine, "Jean Valentine: An Interview by Michael Klein," p. 41.

16. Ibid., p. 39.

17. Jean Valentine, "Anaesthesia," in *Ordinary Things* (New York: Farrar, Straus & Giroux, 1974), p. 8.

18. Valentine, "Jean Valentine: An Interview by Michael Klein," p. 39.

19. Valentine, "The Hallowing of the Everyday," p. 31.

20. Valentine, "Jean Valentine: An Interview by Michael Klein," p. 40.

21. Jean Valentine, "Snow Landscape, in a Glass Globe," in *Home Deep Blue: New and Selected Poems* (Cambridge, Mass.: Alice James Books, 1988), p. 16. Hereafter the title of this collection will be abbreviated as *HDB*, and page numbers will be cited parenthetically in the text.

22. Jean Valentine, "Barrie's Dream, the Wild Geese," in *The River at Wolf* (Cambridge, Mass.: Alice James Books, 1992), p. 27. Hereafter the title of this collection will be abbreviated as *RW*, and page numbers will be cited parenthetically in the text.

23. See Valentine, "Jean Valentine: An Interview by Michael Klein," pp. 39, 40, 42.

24. Valentine, "The Hallowing of the Everyday," p. 29.

CHAPTER 4. THE MASTER OF THE MASTERLESS: JAMES TATE AND THE PLEASURES OF ERROR

1. James Tate, "Autosuggestion: USS North Carolina," in *Worshipful Company of Fletchers* (Hopewell, N.J.: Ecco, 1994), p. 6. Hereafter the title of this collection will be abbreviated as *WCF*, and page numbers will be cited parenthetically in the text.

2. James Tate in *American Poetry Observed: Poets on Their Work*, ed. Joe David Bellamy (Urbana: University of Illinois Press, 1984), p. 261.

3. James Tate, "Awkward Silence," in *Selected Poems* (Hanover, N.H.: Wesleyan University Press, 1991), p. 144. Hereafter the title of this collection will be abbreviated as *SP*, and page numbers will be cited parenthetically in the text.

4. Robinson, Fred Miller. *The Comedy of Language: Studies in Modern Comic Literature* (Amherst: University of Massachusetts Press, 1980), pp. 14–15.

5. James Tate, "First Impressions: Unsurpassed Reader, Award-Winning Writer," *Massachusetts* 3, no. 4 (1992): 4.

6. John Ashbery, "James Tate Wins 1995 Tanning Prize: Largest Annual Literary Prize in the United States," *Poetry Pilot* (winter 1995–96): 1, 31.

7. Paul Breslin, *The Psycho-Political Muse: American Poetry Since the Fifties* (Chicago: University of Chicago Press, 1987), p. 119.

8. Vendler, *Part of Nature, Part of Us: Modern American Poets*, p. 343.

9. James Finn Cotter, "Poetry, Ego and Self," *Hudson Review* 33, no. 1 (1980): 140.

10. William Logan, "Language Against Fear," *Poetry* 130, no. 4 (1997): 221. For a discussion of the failure of ritual in the poetry of James Tate, see Donald Revell's "The Desperate Buck and Wing: James Tate and the Failure of Ritual," *Western Humanities Review* 38, no. 4 (1984): 372–79.

11. Lyotard, *Postmodern Condition*, p. xxv.

12. Mark Jarman, "The Curse of Discursiveness," *Hudson Review* 45, no. 1 (1992): 161.

13. Roland Barthes, *Image-Music-Text*, trans. Stephen Heath (New York: Hill and Wang, 1977), pp. 191–92.

14. James Tate, "The Expert," in *Distance from Loved Ones* (Hanover, N.H.: Wesleyan University Press, 1990), pp. 43–44.

15. James Tate, "Once I Was Young in the Land of Baloney," in *Viper Jazz* (Middletown, Conn.: Wesleyan University Press, 1976), p. 39. Hereafter the title of this collection will be abbreviated as *VJ*, and page numbers will be cited parenthetically in the text.

16. James Tate, "The Boy," in *Absences* (Boston: Atlantic, 1972), p. 16.

17. James Tate, "Little Yellow Leaf," in *The Oblivion Ha-Ha* (Boston: Atlantic, 1970), p. 24.

18. Edward Said, *Beginnings: Intention and Method* (New York: Basic Books, 1975), p. xi.

19. Ibid., p. 34.

20. James Tate, "Missionwork," in *Riven Doggeries* (New York: Ecco, 1979), p. 67.

21. Paul Smith, "We Always Fail—Barthes' Last Writings," *Sub-Stance* 36 (1982): 39.

22. Charles Bernstein, *A Poetics* (Cambridge: Harvard University Press, 1992), pp. 146–47.

CHAPTER 5. FLESHLESS VOICES: LOUISE GLÜCK'S RITUALS OF ABJECTION AND OBLIVION

1. Louise Glück, "Death and Absence," in *The Generation of 2000: Contemporary American Poets*, ed. William Heyen (Princeton, N.J.: Ontario Review Press, 1984) p. 66.

2. Louise Glück, "Invitation and Exclusion," in *Proofs & Theories: Essays on Poetry* (Hopewell, N.J.: Ecco, 1994), p. 120.

3. Elizabeth Dodd, *The Veiled Mirror and the Woman Poet: H.D., Louise Bogan, Elizabeth Bishop, and Louise Glück* (Columbia: University of Missouri Press, 1992), p. 149.

4. See Glück's "Against Sincerity," *American Poetry Review* 22, no. 5 (1993): 27–29.

5. As Lawrence Lipking argues in *Abandoned Women and Poetic Tradition*, "An air of the forbidden, of something potentially explosive or beyond control, hovers around [abandoned women in literature]," p. 2. He refers to the figure of the abandoned woman as "highly subversive," p. 31.

6. Lynn Keller, "'Free / of Blossom and Subterfuge': Louise Glück and the Language of Renunciation," in *World, Self, Poem: Essays on Contemporary Poetry from the "Jubilation of Poets,"* ed. Leonard W. Trawick (Kent, Ohio: Kent State University Press, 1990), p. 120.

7. Ibid., p. 129.

8. Louise Glück, author's note to *The First Four Books of Poems* (Hopewell, N.J.: Ecco, 1995), unpaginated.

9. Louise Glück, "Grandmother in the Garden," in *Firstborn* (New York: New American Library, 1968), p. 18. Hereafter the title of this collection will be abbreviated as *F*, and page numbers will be cited parenthetically in the text.

10. Robert Miklitsch, "Assembling a Landscape: The Poetry of Louise Glück," *Hollins Critic* 19, no. 4 (1982): 3.

11. Louise Glück, "Education of the Poet," in *Proofs & Theories*, p. 10. Text of lecture given at the Solomon R. Guggenheim Museum, New York, 31 January 1989.

12. Louise Glück, "For My Mother," in *The House on Marshland* (New York: Ecco, 1975), p. 6. Hereafter the title of this collection will be abbreviated as *HM*, and page numbers will be cited parenthetically in the text.

13. Glück, "Education of the Poet," p. 10.

14. Ibid., pp. 10–11.

15. Julia Kristeva, *Powers of Horror: An Essay on Abjection*, trans. Leon S. Roudiez (New York: Columbia University Press, 1982), p. 1.

16. Ibid., p. 10.

17. Ibid., p. 1.

18. Ibid., p. 2.

19. Louise Glück, "On Stanley Kunitz," in *Proofs & Theories*, p. 109.

20. Ibid., p. 110.

21. Vendler, *Part of Nature, Part of Us*, p. 303.

22. Miklitsch, "Assembling a Landscape," p. 8.

23. Diane S. Bonds, "Entering Language in Louise Glück's *The House on Marshland*: A Feminist Reading," *Contemporary Literature* 31, no. 1 (1990): 58.

24. Ibid., p. 59.

25. Glück, "Education of the Poet," p. 3.

26. Miklitsch, "Assembling a Landscape," p. 11.

27. Glück, "Education of the Poet," p. 10.

28. Louise Glück, "Autumnal," in *Descending Figure* (New York: Ecco, 1980), p. 37. Hereafter the title of this collection will be abbreviated as *DF*, and page numbers will be cited parenthetically in the text.

29. Greg Kuzma, "Rock Bottom: Louise Glück and the Poetry of Dispassion," *Midwest Quarterly* 24, no. 4 (1983): 472.

30. Ibid., p. 473.

31. Ibid., p. 478.

32. Louise Glück, "The Dreamer and the Watcher," in *Singular Voices: American Poetry Today*, ed. Stephen Berg (New York: Avon, 1985), p. 79.

33. Ibid., p. 80.

34. Louise Glück, "Obstinate Humanity," in *Proofs & Theories*, p. 71.

35. Glück, "The Dreamer and the Watcher," p. 80.

36. Kristeva, *Powers of Horror*, p. 8.

37. Glück, "The Dreamer and the Watcher," pp. 80–81.

38. Louise Glück, introduction to *The Best American Poetry 1993*, ed. Louise Glück, series ed. David Lehman (New York: Collier, 1993), p. xx.

39. Glück, "Education of the Poet," p. 3.

40. Louise Glück, "The Forbidden," *Threepenny Review* 54 (summer 1993): 21.

41. Louise Glück, "The Idea of Courage," in *Proofs & Theories*, p. 27.

42. Louise Glück, "Disruption, Hesitation, Silence," *American Poetry Review* 22, no. 5 (1993): 30.

43. Louise Glück, "On Impoverishment," in *Proofs & Theories*, p. 132.

44. Glück, "The Dreamer and the Watcher," p. 77.

45. Louise Glück, "The Untrustworthy Speaker," in *Ararat* (New York: Ecco, 1990), p. 34. Hereafter the title of this collection will be abbreviated as *A*, and page numbers will be cited parenthetically in the text.

46. Louise Glück, "The Triumph of Achilles," in *The Triumph of Achilles* (New York: Ecco, 1985), p. 16. Hereafter the title of this collection will be abbreviated as *TA*, and page numbers will be cited parenthetically in the text.

47. Eavan Boland, "Making the Difference: Eroticism and Aging in the Work of the Woman Poet," *American Poetry Review* 23, no. 2 (1994): 31.

48. Louise Glück, "The Red Poppy," in *The Wild Iris* (Hopewell, N.J.: Ecco, 1992), p. 29. Hereafter the title of this collection will be abbreviated as *WI*, and page numbers will be cited parenthetically in the text.

49. Louise Glück, "Ithaca," in *Meadowlands* (Hopewell, N.J.: Ecco, 1996), p. 12. Hereafter the title of this collection is abbreviated as *M*, and page numbers will be cited parenthetically in the text.

50. Glück, "Education of the Poet," p. 17.

Works Cited

Ackerman, Duane, "Russell Edson." In *Contemporary Poets*, edited by James Vinson, 426–28. 3d ed. New York: St. Martin's Press, 1980.

Adorno, T. W. *Aesthetic Theory*. Edited by Gretel Adorno and Rolf Tiedemann. Translated by C. Lenhardt. London: Routledge and Kegan Paul, 1984.

Altieri, Charles. *Self and Sensibility in Contemporary American Poetry*. Cambridge: Cambridge University Press, 1984.

Andrews, Tom, ed. *The Points Where All Things Meet: Essays on Charles Wright*. Oberlin, Ohio: Oberlin College Press, 1995.

Ashbery, John. Quoted in "James Tate Wins 1995 Tanning Prize: Largest Annual Literary Prize in the United States." *Poetry Pilot* (winter 1995–96): 1, 31.

Bachelard, Gaston. *The Poetics of Space*. Translated by Maria Jolas. New York: Orion, 1964.

Barthes, Roland. *Image-Music-Text*. Translated by Stephen Heath. New York: Hill and Wang, 1977.

———. *Mythologies*. Translated by Annette Lavers. New York: Farrar, Straus & Giroux, 1972.

Bedient, Calvin. "Slide-Wheeling Around the Curves." In *The Point Where All Things Meet*, edited by Tom Andrews, 39–52. Oberlin, Ohio: Oberlin College Press, 1995.

———. "Tracing Charles Wright." *Parnassus: Poetry in Review* 10, no. 1 (1982): 55–74.

Bellamy, Joe David. *American Poetry Observed: Poets on Their Work*. Urbana: University of Illinois Press, 1984.

Benedikt, Michael. Introduction to *The Prose Poem: An International Anthology*, edited by Michael Benedict, 39–50. New York: Dell, 1976.

Bernstein, Charles. *A Poetics*. Cambridge: Harvard University Press, 1992.

Birkerts, Sven. "Prose Poetry." *Parnassus: Poetry in Review* 15, no. 1 (1989): 163–84.

Blanchot, Maurice. *The Gaze of Orpheus and Other Literary Essays*. Edited by P. Adams Sitney. Translated by Lydia Davis. Barrytown, N.Y.: Station Hill, 1981.

Bloom, Harold. *Figures of Capable Imagination*. New York: Seabury, 1976.

Boland, Eavan. "Making the Difference: Eroticism and Aging in the Work of the Woman Poet." *American Poetry Review* 23, no. 2 (1994): 27–32.

Bond, Bruce. "Metaphysics of the Image in Charles Wright and Paul Cézanne." *Southern Review* 30, no. 2 (1994): 116–25.

Bonds, Diane S. "Entering Language in Louise Glück's *The House on Marshland*: A Feminist Reading." *Contemporary Literature* 31, no. 1 (1990): 58–75.

Booth, Philip. "On Jean Valentine: A Continuum of Turning." *American Poetry Review* 9, no. 1 (1980): 4–6.

Breslin, Paul. *The Psycho-Political Muse: American Poetry Since the Fifties*. Chicago: University of Chicago Press, 1987.

Breton, André. *Manifestoes of Surrealism*. Translated by Richard Seaver and Helen R. Lane. Ann Arbor: University of Michigan Press, 1969.

Brown, Dennis. *The Modernist Self in Twentieth-Century English Literature: A Study in Self-Fragmentation*. New York: St. Martin's Press, 1989.

Caws, Mary Ann. "The Self-Defining Prose Poem: On Its Edge." In *The Prose Poem in France: Theory and Practice*, edited by Mary Ann Caws and Hermine Riffaterre, 180–97. New York: Columbia University Press, 1983.

Cotter, James Finn. "Poetry, Ego and Self." *Hudson Review* 33, no. 1 (1980): 131–45.

Cramer, Steven. "Self-Defense." Review of *The River at Wolf*, by Jean Valentine. *Poetry* 161, no. 3 (1992): 159–81.

DeShazer, Mary K. *Inspiring Women: Reimagining the Muse*. New York: Pergamon, 1986.

Dodd, Elizabeth. *The Veiled Mirror and the Woman Poet: H.D., Louise Bogan, Elizabeth Bishop, and Louise Glück*. Columbia: University of Missouri Press, 1992.

Eagleton, Terry. *Marxism and Literary Criticism*. Berkeley: University of California Press, 1976.

Edson, Russell. *The Clam Theater*. Middletown, Conn.: Wesleyan University Press, 1973.

———. "Counting Sheep." In *Fifty Contemporary Poets: The Creative Process*, edited by Alberta T. Turner, 90–94. New York: McKay, 1977.

———. "The House of Sara Loo." *Parnassus: Poetry in Review* 16, no. 1 (1990): 97.

———. *The Intuitive Journey and Other Works*. New York: Harper, 1976.

———. "One Man's Story." *The Prose Poem: An International Journal* 1 (1992): 29.

———. "Portrait of the Writer as a Fat Man: Some Subjective Ideas or Notions on the Care and Feeding of Prose Poems." In *Claims for Poetry*, edited by Donald Hall, 95–103. Ann Arbor: University of Michigan Press, 1982.

———. "The Prose Poem in America." *Parnassus: Poetry in Review* 5 (1976): 321–25.

———. *The Reason Why the Closet-Man is Never Sad*. Middletown, Conn.: Wesleyan University Press, 1977.

———. *A Stone is Nobody's*. Stanford, Conn.: privately published, 1961.

———. *The Tunnel: Selected Poems*. Oberlin: Oberlin College Press, 1994.

———. *The Very Thing That Happens*. Norfolk, Conn.: New Directions, 1964.

———. *The Wounded Breakfast*. Middletown, Conn.: Wesleyan University Press, 1985.

Finkelstein, Norman. *The Utopian Moment in Contemporary American Poetry*. Lewisburg, Pa.: Bucknell University Press, 1988.

Fitts, Dudley. Foreword to *Dream Barker*. New Haven: Yale University Press, 1965.

Fredman, Stephen. *The Grounding of American Poetry: Charles Olson and the Emersonian Tradition*. Cambridge: Cambridge University Press, 1993.

Friebert, Stuart, and David Young, eds. *Models of the Universe: An Anthology of the Prose Poem*. Oberlin, Ohio: Oberlin College Press, 1995.

Frye, Northrop. *Anatomy of Criticism: Four Essays*. Princeton: Princeton University Press, 1957.

Glück, Louise. "Against Sincerity." *American Poetry Review* 22, no. 5 (1993): 27–29.

———. *Ararat*. New York: Ecco, 1990.

———. "Death and Absence." In *The Generation of 2000: Contemporary American Poets*, edited by William Heyen, 66–68. Princeton, N.J.: Ontario Review Press, 1984.

———. *Descending Figure*. New York: Ecco, 1980.

———. "Disruption, Hesitation, Silence." *American Poetry Review* 22, no. 5 (1993): 30–32.

———. "The Dreamer and the Watcher." In *Singular Voices: American Poetry Today*, edited by Stephen Berg, 75–82. New York: Avon, 1985.

———. *Firstborn*. New York: New American Library, 1968.

———. *The First Four Books of Poems*. Hopewell, N.J.: Ecco, 1995.

———. "The Forbidden." *The Threepenny Review* 54 (summer 1993): 20–21.

———. *The House on Marshland*. New York: Ecco, 1975.

———. Introduction to *The Best American Poetry 1993*, edited by Louise Glück. Series editor David Lehman. New York: Collier, 1993

———. *Meadowlands*. Hopewell, N.J.: Ecco, 1996.

———. *Proofs & Theories: Essays on Poetry*. Hopewell, N.J.: Ecco, 1994.

———. *The Triumph of Achilles*. New York: Ecco, 1985.

———. *The Wild Iris*. Hopewell, N.J.: Ecco, 1992.

Hall, Donald. "On Russell Edson's Genius." *American Poetry Review* 6, no. 5 (1977): 12–13.

Hardy, Donald. "Russell Edson's Humor: Absurdity in a Surreal World." *Studies in American Humor* 6 (1988): 93–100.

Hart, Henry. "Story-Tellers, Myth-Makers, Truth-Sayers." *New England Review* 15, no. 4 (1993): 192–206.

Hawkins, Susan E. "Russell Edson's Fabled World." *American Poetry* 5, no. 3 (1988): 39–52.

Ingersoll, Earl G., Judith Kitchen, and Stan Sanvel Rubin. *The Post-Confessionals: Conversations with American Poets of the Eighties*. Rutherford, N.J.: Fairleigh Dickinson University Press, 1989.

James, William. *The Varieties of Religious Experience: A Study in Human Nature*. New York: Collier, 1961.

Jarman, Mark. "The Curse of Discursiveness." *Hudson Review* 45, no. 1 (1992): 158–66.

Johnson, Barbara. "Disfiguring Poetic Landscape." In *The Prose Poem in France: Theory and Practice,* edited by Mary Ann Caws and Hermine Riffaterre, 79–97. New York: Columbia University Press, 1983.

Keller, Lynn. "'Free / Of Blossom and Subterfuge': Louise Glück and the Language of Renunciation." In *World, Self, Poem: Essays on Contemporary Poetry from the "Jubilation of Poets,"* edited by Leonard W. Trawick, 120–29. Kent, Ohio: Kent State University Press, 1990.

Kennedy, X. J. "A Tenth and Four Fifths." Review of *The Southern Cross*, by Charles Wright. *Poetry* 141 (1983): 349–58.

Kristeva, Julia. *Black Sun: Depression and Melancholia*. Translated by Leon S. Roudiez. New York: Columbia University Press, 1989.

———. *Desire in Language: A Semiotic Approach to Literature and Art*. Edited by Leon S. Roudiez. Translated by Thomas Gora, Alice Jardine, and Leon S. Roudiez. New York: Columbia University Press, 1980.

———. *Powers of Horror: An Essay on Abjection*. Translated by Leon S. Roudiez. New York: Columbia University Press, 1982.

Kuzma, Greg. "Rock Bottom. Louise Glück and the Poetry of Dispassion." *The Midwest Quarterly* 24, no. 4 (1983): 468–81.

Levertov, Denise. Introduction to *The Very Thing That Happens: Fables and Drawings*, by Russell Edson. Norfolk, Conn: New Directions, 1964.

Limehouse, Capers, and Megan Sexton. "Visionary Sceptic: An Interview with Charles Simic." *The Atlanta Review* 2, no. 1 (1995): 23–36.

Lipking, Lawrence. *Abandoned Women and Poetic Tradition*. Chicago: University of Chicago Press, 1988.

Logan, William. "Language Against Fear." *Poetry* 130, no. 4 (1997): 221–29.

Lyotard, Jean-François. *The Postmodern Condition: A Report on Knowledge*. Translated by Geoff Bennington and Brian Massumi. Minneapolis: University of Minnesota Press, 1984.

McBride, Elizabeth. "Charles Wright: An Interview." *Ohio Review* 34 (1985): 14–41.

McClatchy, J. D. "The Art of Poetry XLI: Charles Wright." *Paris Review* 31, no. 113 (1989): 182–221.

McCorkle, James. *The Still Performance: Writing, Self, and Interconnection in Five Postmodern American Poets*. Charlottesville: University Press of Virginia, 1989.

Miklitsch, Robert. "Assembling a Landscape: The Poetry of Louise Glück." *Hollins Critic* 19, no. 4 (1982): 1–13.

Monroe, Jonathan. *A Poverty of Objects: The Prose Poem and the Politics of Genre*. Ithaca: Cornell University Press, 1987.

Parisi, Joseph. "Charles Wright." In *Poets in Person: A Listener's Guide*, 143–55. Chicago: Modern Poetry Association, 1992.

Phillips, Robert. *The Confessional Poets*. Carbondale: Southern Illinois University Press, 1973.

Pinsky, Robert. *The Situation of Poetry: Contemporary Poetry and its Traditions*. Princeton: Princeton University Press, 1976.

Ramke, Bin. "A Gesture of Permission: On Poems in Prose, etc." *Denver Quarterly* 25, no. 4 (1991): 129–35.

Revell, Donald. "The Desperate Buck and Wing: James Tate and the Failure of Ritual." *Western Humanities Review* 38, no. 4 (1984): 372–79.

Robinson, Fred Miller. *The Comedy of Language: Studies in Modern Comic Literature*. Amherst: University of Massachusetts Press, 1980.

Rubin, Stan Sanvel. "Introduction: Beyond the War Zone." In *The Post-Confessionals: Conversations with American Poets of the Eighties*, edited by Earl G. Ingersoll, Judith

Kitchen, and Stan Sanvel Rubin, 11–24. Rutherford, N.J.: Fairleigh Dickinson University Press, 1989.

Said, Edward. *Beginnings: Intention and Method.* New York: Basic Books, 1975.

St. John, David. Foreword to *Country Music: Selected Early Poems,* by Charles Wright. 2d ed. Hanover, N.H.: Wesleyan University Press, 1991.

Shetley, Vernon. *After the Death of Poetry: Poet and Audience in Contemporary America.* Durham, N.C.: Duke University Press, 1993.

Smith, Paul. "We Always Fail—Barthes' Last Writings," *Sub-Stance* 36 (1982): 39–40.

Stewart, Susan. *Nonsense: Aspects of Intertextuality in Folklore and Literature.* Baltimore: Johns Hopkins University Press, 1979.

Tate, James. *Absences.* Boston: Atlantic, 1972.

———. *Constant Defender.* New York: Ecco, 1983.

———. *Distance from Loved Ones.* Hanover, N.H.: Wesleyan University Press, 1990.

———. "First Impressions: Unsurpassed Reader, Award-Winning Writer." *Massachusetts* 3, no. 4 (1992): 4.

———. *The Lost Pilot.* New Haven: Yale University Press, 1967.

———. *The Oblivion Ha-Ha.* Boston: Atlantic, 1970.

———. *Riven Doggeries.* New York: Ecco, 1979.

———. *Selected Poems.* Hanover, N.H.: Wesleyan University Press, 1991.

———. *Viper Jazz.* Middletown, Conn.: Wesleyan University Press, 1976.

———. *Worshipful Company of Fletchers.* Hopewell, N.J.: Ecco, 1994.

Tillinghast, Richard. "From 'An Elegist's New England, A Buddhist's Dante.'" In *The Point Where All Things Meet: Essays on Charles Wright,* edited by Tom Andrews, 195–97. Oberlin, Ohio: Oberlin College Press, 1995.

Valentine, Jean. *Dream Barker.* New Haven: Yale University Press, 1965.

———. "The Hallowing of the Everyday." In *Acts of Mind: Conversations with Contemporary Poets,* ed. Richard Jackson, 27–31. Tuscaloosa: University of Alabama Press, 1983.

———. *Home Deep Blue: New and Selected Poems.* Cambridge, Mass.: Alice James Books, 1988.

———. "Jean Valentine: An Interview by Michael Klein." *American Poetry Review* 20, no. 4 (1991): 39–44.

———. *The Messenger.* New York: Farrar, Straus & Giroux, 1979.

———. *Ordinary Things.* New York: Farrar, Straus & Giroux, 1974.

———. *Pilgrims.* New York: Farrar, Straus & Giroux, 1969.

———. *The River at Wolf.* Cambridge, Mass.: Alice James Books, 1992.

Vendler, Helen. *The Breaking of Style: Hopkins, Heaney, Graham.* Cambridge: Harvard University Press, 1995.

———. *Part of Nature, Part of Us: Modern American Poets.* Cambridge: Harvard University Press, 1980.

Williamson, Alan. *Introspection and Contemporary Poetry.* Cambridge: Harvard University Press, 1984.

Wright, Charles. *Black Zodiac*. New York: Farrar, Straus & Giroux, 1997.

———. *Chickamauga*. New York: Farrar, Straus & Giroux, 1995.

———. *Country Music: Selected Early Poems*. 2d ed. Hanover, N.H.: Wesleyan University Press, 1991.

———. "Halflife / A Commonplace Notebook." *Field* 36 (spring 1987): 18–34.

———. "Improvisations on Form and Measure." *Ohio Review* 38 (1987): 20–24.

———. "An Interview with Charles Wright." Interview by Sherod Santos. *The Missouri Review* 10, no. 1 (1987): 73–95.

———. *The Other Side of the River*. New York: Random House, 1984.

———. *Quarter Notes: Improvisations and Interviews*. Ann Arbor: University of Michigan Press, 1995.

———. *The World of the Ten Thousand Things: Poems, 1980–1990*. New York: Farrar, Straus & Giroux, 1990.

Index

159